Bicycling Books®

# BASIC RIDING TECHNIQUES

*by the editors of **Bicycling**® magazine*

Printed in the United States of America on recycled paper, containing a high percentage of de-inked fiber.

Cover photograph by Steve Firebaugh

Book series design by K. A. Schell

**Library of Congress Cataloging in Publication Data**
Main entry under title:

Basic riding techniques.

    (Bicycling books series)
    SUMMARY: Guide to efficient and effective bicycling, discussing such techniques as cadence, gear shifting, uphill and downhill riding, and wet weather biking.
    1. Cycling. [1. Bicycles and bicycling] I. Bicycling (Emmaus, Pa.) II. Series.

GV1041.B35    796.6    79-9423
ISBN 0-87857-284-8  paperback

      8   10  9  7       paperback

# Contents

# Introduction

Recently, while sitting on my front porch, I saw what appeared to be a father and daughter cycling. They were in single file, riding against traffic. While I am no expert in fitting bikes, I immediately sensed something was wrong. The father seemed to be riding a bike a couple of sizes too small, as he was hardly able to extend his legs. On the other hand, the girl seemed unable to sit in the saddle and still pedal; so she was standing on the pedals, rocking back and forth, following this adult headlong into traffic.

So there they were, riding against traffic on ill-fitting bikes. If the situation were not so dangerous, it would have been laughable.

After I had fumed a bit over the safety question, I laid the matter down to inexperience. No cyclist with knowledge of the machine would make these mistakes. Still, this got me thinking about the complexity of the relationship between bicycle and rider.

Few people would argue that the "bicycle as a toy" idea is not a pervasive theme in our culture, though this perception is fortunately changing. Even so, the bike is too frequently considered something you buy for the kids at Christmas.

But there is a kind of wrong-thinking about cycling, especially with regard to techniques, throughout the sport. I recall a young woman racer I spoke to recently who claimed that "I had been pedaling incorrectly for about four years until Eddy Borysewicz (national coach) showed me what I was doing wrong."

According to Peter R. Cavanagh, Professor of Biomechanics at Pennsylvania State University, "There are a great many myths and half-truths to be found in the cycling world primarily because some aspects of cycling have not been subjected to serious research." Contrary to popular opinion Cavanagh feels that cycling is a "complex skill" involving more than keeping the bike stable and traveling in a reasonably straight line. "Riding a bike in such a way to insure efficient pedaling," Cavanagh asserted, "is of equal

1

importance to the commuter, the tourist and the racer. The way in which power is dissipated will influence who will win the race or who will be able to complete a tour with least fatigue." And, he added, "many things keep us from riding efficiently."

For example, some people are quite cavalier when it comes to bicycle seat height. "Few people realize," says Cavanagh, "that when you move the seatpost an innocent inch or two, up or down, you are changing the action of every muscle in the lower limb which is involved in the pedaling action." If the seat is in the incorrect position, more oxygen must be consumed and the work becomes harder, causing a drop in efficiency, perhaps as much as 10 percent.

"If the seat height is wrong," he continues, "you will be riding dangerously from a number of viewpoints. Firstly, if the seat is too low, it's unlikely that your control of the bicycle will be affected. But it is likely that you'll be leading yourself toward some nagging ache and pain that's not going to go away as long as your seat is badly adjusted. Now, at the other end, if the seat is too high it's going to cause you to move excessively from one side of the bicycle to the other. It's possible that it will affect your control of the machine."

The vision of the well-trained cyclist pedaling down the road probably strikes us as an image of beauty and efficiency. Not so, according to Cavanagh, at least the efficiency part. Prodded by his curiosity, he tested, in his Biomechanics Laboratory, a number of healthy individuals who regularly cycled around campus. To his surprise, he discovered that some cyclists did twice as much work with one leg as the other. Ironically, when he tested the same individuals the following day, he found the opposite might be true.

So, contrary to popular thinking, most cyclists probably don't cycle symmetrically; that is, apply equal pressure with both legs. They tend to overuse one leg on a particular day. According to Cavanagh, "The results of these experiments carry implications that most of us who ride bikes do so, to some extent, asymmetrically. Taken to extremes this imbalance could result in early fatigue in the muscles and inefficient pedaling. It may well be of value during training rides for the cyclist to deliberately overemphasize the action of each leg for a period of time to become more aware of what asymmetry feels like. Also, during 'off the bike' training sessions, effort should be made to exercise both legs; weight training is particularly useful here since limbs can be both tested and trained individually."

In this researcher's opinion, there are numerous "stampers" among cycling enthusiasts who apply pedal force in only one direction. "You may be exerting," he writes, "a larger force on the pedal than any known cyclist before you, but unless the force is in the right direction, it will not necessarily result in large propulsion forces at the wheel."

Experienced cyclists, of course, know this and, accordingly, employ the practice of ankling which permits them to exert maximum useful force on the pedals by changing the position of the ankle joint. Most of the cycling books suggest that, as you come across the top of the pedal stroke, you drop the heel; then you attempt to push the pedal horizontally through the top part of the stroke. Instead of stamping down, you push across the stroke.

Cavanagh feels that such advice is laudable but anatomically such a "posture is extremely difficult for most of us to achieve, indeed impossible for some of us. We did a study on racing cyclists with our equipment on the bicycle which can measure the orientation of the pedal. We actually measured the angles that the foot did make to the vertical throughout the pedal. We found that what was being said in the book(s) was totally wrong. These cyclists we tested were just not pedaling by dropping the heel on the way across. They were doing exactly the opposite. They were dropping the toe on the way across the top of the cycle and, in that manner, they were able to achieve that change in orientation of the force vector. And so I would caution the average cyclist about looking up in a manual on how to orient the foot and trying to duplicate it because there really are some wrong ideas that have been transmitted in the past. I think that this is an extremely good example of where sport has suffered from opinion rather than evidence. They are based on what I call armchair biomechanics."

In his pursuit of fact rather than fancy, Cavanagh has enlisted the aid of an on-line computer in his lab, hooked up to a bike, which provides graphic printouts regarding a cyclist's pedaling symmetry, ankling style, torque, crank angle and other factors. During a recent trip to Pennsylvania State University, I had the opportunity to visit the Biomechanics Lab and get an abbreviated computer printout on my riding style. The results, while incomplete, were absolutely fascinating to me. I had always thought that I had a smooth, pedaling action, but the printouts graphically showed that such was not the case. On the contrary, I tended to be an impulsive pedaler with my right foot because as I got to bottom dead center I tended to apply an extra effort. On the other hand, the printout showed my left foot pedaling motion fairly consistently through both the recovery and propulsion stages. I couldn't argue with the evidence. I had a short, impulsive stroke with my right foot and a more even, long stroke with my left.

Furthermore, I discovered, again graphically, that my style of ankling was close to the test results outlined above. Cavanagh is the

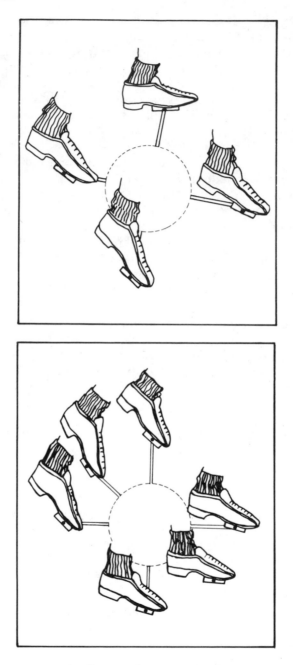

Cycling literature reports that people pedal with their feet at angles shown in the top diagram. Biomechanical researchers after high-speed filming report that actual ankling angles are far different (bottom diagram). All of which proves that armchair research is often faulty.

first to acknowledge that many of his findings are at this time tentative. But not for long. He will be testing a control group of cyclists in the near future, large enough so that he will be able to make some appropriate generalizations about riding styles. Concurrently, one of his graduate students, Mario LaFortune, is performing similar tests on the efficiency of toe clips. Both researchers vigorously question the popular notion that toe clips increase pedaling efficiency anywhere from 50 to 100 percent.

He is also testing, for the Consumer Product Safety Commission, the amount of pedal slippage that occurs in typical situations where cyclists are not wearing toe clips for one reason or another. He is interested in finding out where the pedal slip most likely occurs in the pedaling cycle, and whether this occurs under certain combinations of materials used for shoe and for the pedal surface. Cavanagh believes this an extremely important area of research, particularly for casual riders and commuters who are reluctant to wear toe clips because of the difficulty they might have in getting out of them. Pedal slippage, which can result in loss of bike control and possible leg injury, is another area where Cavanagh wants to make some concrete recommendations to the general public.

More and more people are realizing that they can't just hop on a bike and hope to pedal efficiently and effectively. There is no reason to think that a person instinctively knows how to ride uphill and downhill, to travel in a pack, and to get maximum benefit from toe clips.

Bicycle riding and handling, like driving a car, is a learned activity. An individual must know how to put the body into a proper relationship with the bike. To get the most from the bike, one must understand cadence and gearing and must know how to get the most out of each pedal revolution.

Veteran cyclists will frequently claim that much of the pleasure from cycling comes after the basic riding techniques have been mastered to such a degree that they are second nature. Gear-shifting is an automatic response; pedal cadence is as regular and predictable as a pulse.

The purpose of this book is to help make the basic and essential riding techniques automatic activities. When cycling is second nature, much of the fun begins.

James C. McCullagh
Editor
*Bicycling* magazine

# The Proper Cadence

## Raymond J. Adams

When reading cycling books and magazines, you inevitably come across the subject of cadence. It is usually covered in a few paragraphs, rarely more than half a page. You will usually be told that in order to ride well you have to establish a steady rate of pedaling; this is known as maintaining the proper cadence. Excluding racing, a good rate or cadence should be between 60 and 85 revolutions per minute (rpm).

While most writers will suggest that you try to establish a cadence closer to 85 than to 60, they will also agree that there is no absolutely right cadence. You have to try and find a rate best suited to your ability.

But cadence can be more than just a basic riding skill. It can teach you some things even as you learn it. Once you have learned it, it can teach you still other things. However, cadence is one of those riding skills that is easy to explain and understand but not quite as easy to learn.

Whether you consciously try to establish a regular cadence of your own or just sort of work your way into it by accident, you will probably go through several stages. During your first few rides, you will have no regular cadence at all, and you shouldn't try to establish one just then. In order to learn cadence, you have to understand gearing in general, and you have to understand the specific gearing arrangement you have on your own bicycle. If you are still at the stage where you never know quite what you are going to get when you shift, spend some more time learning the gears on your bicycle. You don't have to wait until you are proficient in their use to start learning cadence, but each gear shift shouldn't be a surprise, either.

Once you start trying to learn cadence, you will have to think about it all the time. As soon as your attention drifts, so will your rpm. Then you get to the point where you only have to think about it occasionally. Finally, it becomes an automatic process where you always maintain a steady cadence but never think about it any more. As a matter of fact, once you have really established a cadence of your own, you may temporarily find it as hard to raise or lower it as it once was to maintain it.

Learning how to maintain cadence goes hand in hand with learning how to use the gears. Every time you get to a rise, a grade or a hill, you have to shift down to the right gear to make pedaling easy enough to let you maintain your regular cadence. That takes practice. What you should try to do first is learn to maintain a regular cadence in *one* gear under *one unchanging set of conditions*. Once you have learned that, you can expand your skills.

Carefully set up the conditions under which you will practice. Select a road that is straight, level, wide and as free of traffic and traffic signals as possible. I suggest a straight road because it gives you the feeling of distance that you never get when you ride around in circles. If you haven't taken many rides, plan your ride in terms of time rather than miles. You may not know how far you can ride, but you should have a good idea of how long you can ride. Make sure the weather is good and there is not too much wind. Be rested when you start. Make up your mind that this ride is a learning session. You are not taking it to sightsee or improve your physical condition. Concentrate on cadence.

Select a gear that seems comfortable and start off. Check your rpm with your watch to make sure that you are somewhere in the 60 to 85 rpm range. Concentrate on trying to hold your cadence at a rate that you can maintain for some time. It is right at this point that you should rid yourself of the commonly believed myth that you are not really cycling unless you are in a gear where you are laboring. Making cycling easy is the reason for having ten speeds.

Right off you may find that it not only takes practice to maintain a regular cadence, but it often takes time to discover which is the right gear for you even under the simplest circumstances. A gear which seemed just right at first can be exhaustingly difficult two or three miles later. You will have to experiment until you find that right combination. Even if the gear you started off with seems right, shift up and down now and then. You may find one that is even better. And every time you start to tire, remember that there are several possible reasons, not just one. You may be pedaling too fast, and/or you may be in too high a gear, or you may have ridden enough for one day.

Take practice runs as often as you can. You may be surprised at how quickly you begin to fall into a regular pedaling pattern. You are on your way to the time you can maintain a regular cadence without having to think about it.

You should now start learning another basic skill and that is learning to interpret pedal pressure. Once you have established the right gear ratio-rpm combination, start paying attention to how your feet feel against the pedals. After awhile, you will be able to read even the slightest change in street grade. Near my home is a street that I would swear is flat. Pedal pressure tells me that it is not. Every experienced rider who rides in hilly country will tell you that there will be times when your eyes will tell you that the road ahead is level or downhill, but your feet will tell you that it is uphill. Your feet will be right. Eventually, you will be able to feel even the subtlest changes in the road surface or grade.

Once you have the proper gear ratio-rpm-pedal pressure combination for a ride on level ground, you are ready for the next two steps. They are steps that can be learned simultaneously.

Now that you have a basic cadence that you can do under simple, unvarying conditions, your next step is to start practicing under changing conditions such as riding up grades or hills, into the wind, or with a loaded bicycle.

As soon as you reach a rise or grade, the increase in pedal pressure will let you know immediately. It will tell you that you may have to gear down or you will burn out. The normal reaction is to slow down your cadence. Hold it and gear down instead until a feeling of normal pedal pressure returns.

There is only one time you should slow down your cadence. If you hit a steep grade and find that it is still too hard to hold cadence in your lowest gear, then slow your rpm down. After all, that's all you have left that you can do. Maintaining a steady cadence is a good, smart way of riding, but it's not a holy law.

Even without consciously thinking about any of these things, you would probably learn them all eventually, anyway. But it is not as easy as it sounds. I have seen any number of riders sitting exhausted on the side of an uphill road because they couldn't read pedal pressure. If they could, they would have known that it had been telling them in a very loud voice to gear down or slow down or else. Many beginners will also have troubles when going on their first rides, even easy ones, with a riding club. As soon as they hit an overpass, or a mild, block-long grade, they fall behind. They either take the grade in too high a gear or spend too much time searching for the right gear.

The most important argument for consciously learning gear ratio-rpm-pedal pressure combinations is that it is important to learn them all at about the same time. Because you now want to get all three to the point where you do them without thinking, just as you shift, use the brakes or step on the gas when driving your car. If you have to think about them all the time, you are too busy to enjoy the ride.

Part of a ride I took recently was through hill country. None of the hills were very high, just high and steep enough to make me shift now and then. When I finished the ride, I knew that I had shifted gears a number of times, but I didn't have the faintest idea of when or how often. I had been too busy enjoying the ride. I had let my feet do the thinking.

Try to establish a basic gear-cadence combination. Use it to teach yourself the proper pedal pressure. Use this knowledge to help you when you practice on varied terrain. Then take what you have learned and teach yourself to use it without thinking about it.

# Efficient Cycling

## Raymond J. Adams

You might say that efficient cycling is that kind of riding where the rider gets a maximum return in terms of speed and/or distance for the energy expended. But that definition has its limits. It can be equally true to say that a cyclist is riding efficiently when using the cadence, gearing and other techniques best suited to immediate and overall needs on the ride.

Your motives and needs for a specific ride should always override everything else. The cadence and gear you may use in a 10-mile high-speed sprint are not the ones best suited to a leisurely 50-mile tour of the countryside. That's where you go from learning cadence to learning pacing. Decisions about pacing are usually made by your mind and not your body.

During the summer I learned to ride, I had managed to extend my one-day range to about 30 to 35 miles. I decided to stretch it to 50 miles. It seemed like a reasonable increase. Yet, for the first couple of 50-mile rides, I found myself burning out badly the last 10 miles. Why? My body couldn't tell me. As a matter of fact, it had felt terrific the first 20 or 25 miles. All it could tell me was that it was suddenly collapsing at the 40-mile mark. It couldn't tell me why. It was only when I solved the problem of the 40-mile sag that I really began to understand pacing.

I was still a beginning rider, and each week my legs were growing stronger. By coincidence, I had increased my normal cruising gear on the same trip that I went from 35 to 50 miles. I was riding the first 25 miles in one gear setting higher than ever before. I would tire somewhat and have to drop down one gear. The gear I dropped into had previously been my regular cruising gear.

My body had been of no help in giving me information. It felt very strong when I started. The psychological boost I had gotten from going faster had only blurred my judgment, not improved it. All I got the first half of the trip were good messages. But that's where I was making my mistake.

Increasing my riding range and using a higher gear all at once had been too much of a change. By using that higher gear at first, I was making an error at the beginning of the ride. But I wasn't paying the penalty until 40 miles and several hours later. On my next 50-mile ride, I began in the gear I had previously used. My problem was solved.

There is no magic cadence-gear ratio combination. It differs with each individual. If you are just beginning to ride, it can change with almost every ride before it eventually begins to stabilize.

Compare the body and arm positions of the two riders. The rider on the left is in the more streamlined position which permits more efficient cycling.

So try to think of cycling efficiently as the practice of selecting the proper pace and gear for a specific ride. This avoids the error of thinking that there is only one gear ratio-cadence combination that you have to stick to, no matter what. An efficient, well-paced ride is one where you compromise. No matter how good you feel at the start of a long ride, you have to hold it down to a pace that will let you finish the second half of it. If you can't find a pace that satisfies both requirements, you are probably on the wrong ride.

On longer rides, there is no substitute for a good, steady pace to cover the miles. But once you have learned to ride well, there is no law that says there is only one way to ride or that you must set a certain pace for all rides. Let me give you an example of how varied a ride can be and still be an efficiently ridden one.

Recently, I took my car to a garage for repairs. I was told that it would take three hours. Having anticipated the wait, I had brought along my bicycle. I decided to ride around at random.

Nearby was an exclusive residential district. I decided to ride through it. I wanted to go very slowly and see as much as possible. I shifted up a couple of gears and slowed my cadence to about 30 rpm. The high gear setting kept my cadence down without my having to think about it. This mode of operation was the best for the moment because it let me ride with a minimum of attention paid to pacing and cycling. I was able to see more as I rode. In objective terms, I probably was not riding efficiently. But for my needs of the moment, I was.

When I had ridden through the area, I decided to ride to a local park five miles away. I dropped down the two gears and picked up my cadence to my normal 72 rpm. I made the trip at what was my proper cruising speed. For my needs of the moment, I was again cycling efficiently.

Once in the park, I decided to climb a nearby 800-foot hill. I had been up the hill 50 times. Normally, I would ride up as fast as I could. On that day I didn't feel like hurrying. I shifted down to my bottom gear of 38 and pedaled slowly up the road. Because of this lower-than-normal gear, I didn't have to use the lower handlebars. I was able to look around at the view, the trees, the squirrels, and enjoy the light breeze. I didn't think about technique, time or anything else. I was riding efficiently because I was riding in a manner that suited my immediate needs.

I rode to the top and down the other side. That was when I discovered that my watch had stopped. I was 15 miles from the garage, and it closed in about an hour. Half of the trip had a lot of traffic and traffic lights.

If I had not understood pacing and my own limitations, I would have either geared up or increased my cadence while in my cruising gear. But I knew myself well enough to know that if I did that, I would spend half my time racing along and the other half barely moving while I caught my breath. I would burn out before I arrived at the garage.

Instead, I dropped down one gear and greatly increased my cadence to an rpm I knew I could maintain for 15 miles in that specific gear. All I saw on the whole trip was my front wheel, the traffic and the traffic signals. The red lights I hit gave me enough of a breather for the pace I set for myself.

I burnt out just as I arrived at the garage—in time. For the purpose I had in mind, I had ridden efficiently.

There is no question that learning to ride well requires discipline and a lot of vigorous cycling. There is no argument that to ride efficiently, you must learn to get the most out of your bicycle for the amount of effort used to move it. For many riders that is enough. They get all the satisfaction they need from going the farthest and the fastest with the least effort.

But once you have learned to ride well, look for cycling efficiency in your own way. Don't let anyone tell you that their way is the only way, and if you don't do as they do, you are wrong. Ride for yourself. Any efforts on your part to conform to someone else's ideas will eventually discourage you from riding.

Truly efficient cycling cannot be measured only in miles covered or energy expended. It is only when you receive the greatest amount of satisfaction for the amount of energy expended that you have learned to cycle efficiently.

# Introduction to Gears

## Raymond J. Adams

The one part of a 10-speed bicycle that can be hard to understand is the gearing system. If you don't understand it thoroughly, you cannot use it effectively. Unless you can use it effectively, you will never ride well.

Before speaking about the specifics of the gearing system, let's go over it in general. It consists of the following: two control levers, cables from the control levers to the front and rear derailleurs, front and rear derailleurs, bicycle chain, and the front and rear sets of toothed wheels.

There are two basic kind of control levers. One is attached to the bicycle frame. The other has the levers attached to the tips of the turned-down handlebars. The type attached to the bicycle frame is by far the most common type.

You can get into some highly emotional arguments about the relative values of the two. But unless you become involved in racing, one is as good as the other when starting out.

The heart of the gearing system consists of the two toothed wheels by the pedals and the five on the rear wheel. When talking about the size of these wheels, you never refer to their diameter. Their size is measured by the number of teeth they have. The teeth are always the same distance apart since they must be able to accept the bicycle chain. If you ask a cyclist the size of one of these wheels, they will not say, "It is 8 inches in diameter." Instead they will tell you, "It has 48 teeth."

These wheels have a bewildering number of names. I have heard them referred to as chainwheels, freewheels, cogs, sprockets, cams, and gears. However, the two toothed wheels by the pedals are usually referred to as chainwheels and the five on the rear wheel as sprockets. A set of five sprockets is a sprocket cluster.

When cyclists talk about gearing, they also refer to the rear wheel as the freewheel because it will continue to turn if you stop pedaling or even if you backpedal.

The first few times you use the terms chainwheel and freewheel, they can be confusing. Although it is redundant, I will refer to them as the front chainwheel and the rear freewheel.

When talking about different gear settings, the two terms used are gear ratios and inches. However, most cyclists will simply use the word gear instead of saying gear ratio. I was going to explain gear ratios in detail at this point until I realized it would take the rest of the chapter. Instead, I will just say that it is a measuring system that helps you to know which gear to use in certain circumstances. Should you wish to know more about the subject, ask an experienced cyclist.

The term "inches," when used to refer to a gear size, doesn't give you any useful information that will help you ride better. Although you may read about or hear cyclists mentioning a gear (ratio) of 72 inches or 94 inches, I will simply say 72 gear or 94 gear.

Gear ratios range from about 28 to 105. In order to make sense out of these numbers, you have to know what they mean and how to shift on your bicycle so you can use them. It might, for example, just have a low gear of 38 and a high gear of 96.

Here is an approximate breakdown of the uses of these various gears or gear ratios:

28 gear to 35 gear: These are very low gears. They are meant primarily for very steep hills or touring in hilly country with a loaded bicycle.

35 gear to 44 gear: These are generally used for riding uphill.

44 gear to 60 gear: These are meant for use on milder uphill grades, riding into the wind or riding a loaded bicycle on level ground.

60 gear to 85 gear: These are generally used for riding on level ground.

85 gear to 105 gear: These are very high gears used by strong riders for high-speed riding or by average riders when going downhill.

These figures are no help unless you can apply them to your own bicycle. So let's look at the front chainwheels and the rear sprocket cluster.

The front chainwheels are larger (have more teeth) than the rear sprockets. Normally, you will not find a 10-speed bicycle with a small chainwheel that has much less than 36 teeth or a large chainwheel with more than 52. On the rear sprocket cluster, the smallest sprocket usually has 14 teeth. The largest sprocket you can presently get has 34 teeth. The other three sprockets are spaced out more or less evenly between the largest and the smallest. Just remember that a sprocket with 34 teeth is very large. On many bicycles, the largest sprocket may have only 26, 28, or 31 teeth.

Just knowing the size of the chainwheels and the sprockets still does not give you the gear or gear ratio. In order to determine that, you have to use a formula.

Suppose you have a large front chainwheel of 50 teeth and one of the rear sprockets has 25 teeth. If the chain were on these two, what gear would you be in? Here is the formula to find out:

$$\frac{\text{teeth on chainwheel}}{\text{teeth on rear sprocket}} \times \text{diameter of wheel} = \text{gear ratio}$$

Putting this into numbers we get: $\dfrac{50}{25} \times 27 = 54$

Your bicycle is in 54 gear. Using this same formula, you can find out the gear ratios for all ten combinations. Just count the teeth on the two chainwheels and the five rear sprockets and use the formula. Once you have worked out the gear or gear ratios for all ten combinations, you may often discover that you don't have a 10-speed bicycle after all. You may have only an 8- or 9-speed machine.

In the above example, a larger front chainwheel of 50 teeth and a rear sprocket with 25 teeth gave you a gear ratio of 54. What if the smaller front chainwheel has 40 teeth and the next smallest rear sprocket has 20 teeth? If you use this combination, you get the following:

$$\frac{40}{20} \times 27 = 54 \text{ gear}$$

This gives you precisely the same gear as the 50–25 combination. At best, you have a 9-speed machine.

Is it necessary to insist on a set of gear combinations that give you ten speeds? (Not if you have all the gears you need with eight or nine speeds.) What is the ideal set of gears? Well, theoretically, the ideal arrangement would be one where you have a good low gear, a good high gear, no overlapping gears and where the percentage of difference between all gears is small and consistently the same.

This theoretical idea is easier to define than to achieve. In the first place, it is very difficult to get the right combination of front chainwheels and rear sprockets that will meet all of these goals.

There is another reason. This theoretical ideal may not meet your specific needs. The idea of ten evenly spaced gears, for example, is very attractive, intellectually. It looks so orderly. But if you do a lot of hill climbing or touring with heavy loads, you may want more than the usual number of very low gears. If you ride almost exclusively in level country with little wind on an unloaded bicycle, you may want the majority of gears between 69 and 85 gear. There is no reason to carry around a set of gears you never use simply for the sake of having a mathematically pleasing gear arrangement. When selecting a set of gears, consider your individual needs.

It is also possible to have only an 8- or 9-speed bicycle even when the gears do not overlap.

Let's take an imaginary beginning cyclist who lives in the Louisiana Gulf Coast country, which is about as flat as you can get. Let's also imagine that the bicycle has a low gear of 33 and a high gear of 104. At most, it is an 8-speed bicycle. A 33 gear is just too low for level riding. You are barely moving, no matter how fast you spin the pedals. It is like pedaling in thin air. Our cyclist will burn out in a very short time.

The 104 gear is also wasted on the bicycle. It is just too high for our beginner to use. The first bicycle I owned had a high gear of 96. Just by accident I shifted into that gear the first week I began to ride. I couldn't even turn the pedals. I fell off the bicycle.

So get gears in a range that you can use, not in a range that a very strong rider uses, or one that looks great on paper.

Sally Ann Shenk

**Shifting with the fingertips does not provide maximum leverage.**

Sally Ann Shenk

**You can get a surer, firmer shift by using the palm of your hand.**

When practicing using the gears, there are several things to remember. Don't shift gears unless you are moving. Otherwise, you may damage the derailleurs, teeth or chain. The less tension the chain is under, the easier it is to shift gears. The easiest time is when you are coasting or pedaling on level ground. The hardest time is when you are moving uphill. Avoid it when you can. When you see a hill coming, shift down before you reach it.

Shift gears every chance you get, even at the slightest grade and even if you do not really need to. This will help you in two areas. It will help you to become familiar with the specific gears you have and what they can and cannot do. It will also teach you to shift smoothly. The rider who has never learned to shift properly spends half a block moving the shift levers hoping to find the correct gear.

If you are having trouble remembering which way the chain has to move to shift up or down, use this rule of thumb. Everytime you use the derailleur to shift the chain away from the side of the bicycle, you are shifting to a higher gear. Moving the chain closer to the bicycle is shifting down to a lower gear.

If you have regular levers on your bicycle, remember this rule. When they are pointing straight up, you are in a high gear. When you push them down, you are going into lower gears. As to which lever controls the front and which the rear, remember that the right one controls the rear derailleur. Just keep repeating, "right rear, right rear" to your self until you always remember it.

# Basic Gear Shifting

## Raymond J. Adams

Almost every weekend I take part of my Saturday or Sunday ride with beginning cyclists who want tips on riding. Whatever other problems they have, there are three which keep coming up.

Too many act as though they are riding 1-speed bicycles. They never think about the gears until pedaling becomes so hard they cannot move forward. Because they use the gears so seldom, they don't often shift properly as they are not sure just what they have available.

If you are just starting to ride, use the gears constantly. Shift every time you come to the slightest or shortest grade. Try to shift into a gear that will keep the pedal pressure the same. The idea is to make shifting as natural as pedaling. Later on, as your strength and experience grow, you may laugh at how often you shifted gears over certain routes. But if that constant shifting really taught you to use the gears, then it was worth it. Many a rider trying to keep up with others has fallen behind the group trying to muscle his/her way up every grade while the others are taking advantage of the gears. If you own a 10-speed bicycle, learn to use the gears when you need them.

Another problem occurs for many beginners when they don't look ahead. If you see two or three successive rises separated by short, level stretches, don't attack the first one so vigorously or in such a high gear that you don't have anything left for the next ones. Even a very mild grade can wear you down if it is long enough. Learn to shift down as soon as it gets difficult.

Very often, riders who do try to shift down wait too long. Always shift before you reach the grade. The more tension the chain is under, the more difficult it is to shift. I always look ahead while I can still see the point where the road starts to rise. I will pick something out like a bush or a tree at the place I plan to shift. When I reach that point, I shift.

If you don't get into the habit of doing this, you will often find yourself halfway up a grade in the impossible position where you cannot shift gears and you cannot continue to pedal. The only thing left is to try to fall off your bicycle as gracefully and safely as possible.

Remember that one of the skills you want to acquire is the ability to level out the minor grades, rises and bumps in the road, to turn it into a smooth, level ribbon over which you can move easily and steadily, mile after mile. Learning to use the gears and learning to look ahead are skills that help you do this. Endurance and strength-building techniques can come later.

# Using Toe Clips

## Judy Tate and Gail Shierman

Bicycling literature has often emphasized that the use of toe clips can greatly aid the bicyclist. Some say that the correct use of toe clips can improve pedaling efficiency by as much as 50 percent.

Logically, it is assumed that additional muscles can be utilized on the pedal upstroke, thereby relieving those used in the corresponding downstroke. Recently, a study was conducted at the Texas Woman's University, Denton, Texas, to compare some muscle patterns elicited while pedaling with toe clips as well as when toe clips were not used. An electromyograph, which showed electrical records of muscle activity, was used for this comparison. A skilled bicyclist rode on exercise rollers while readings from four muscles were obtained. These muscles were the tibialis anterior located on the front of the lower leg, the gastrocnemius commonly known as the calf muscle and found on the back of the lower leg, the rectus femoris on the front of the thigh, and the biceps femoris on the back of the thigh and referred to as the hamstring.

The readings were transformed into proportions of a circle to represent muscle activity of the four muscles tested in their respective positions of the pedal revolution. Electromyographic recordings were also inspected to note any marked differences in pedaling without toe clips.

It is evident that when toe clips are used, the tibialis anterior is working for a longer period of time than when toe clips are not used. The tibialis anterior, being an ankle flexor, pulls up on the toe clip as the foot ankles into position for the downstroke. This pattern is absent when toe clips are not used. The gastrocnemius, biceps femoris, and rectus femoris were working also for a longer period of time when toe clips were used.

These findings imply that the additional duration of effort by the tibialis anterior when toe clips are used relieves other muscles usually associated with cycling fatigue. Hopefully, some of this assistance goes to the rectus femoris and other muscles on the front of the thigh. When toe clips were used, the intensity of effort of the tibialis anterior was greater also. This is easily explained by the fact that the toe clip strap provides a resistance on the upstroke.

The gastrocnemius is working also for a longer period of time and with greater intensity when toe clips are used. This muscle helps flex the knee during the upstroke, and therefore probably takes some of the load off the hamstrings which also flex the knee and usually fatigue early.

This preliminary study was designed to get a general idea regarding the trends of muscle patterns with and without toe clips. From our information it would be impossible to state that toe clips improve pedaling efficiency by a set percentage.

# Uphill Riding

## Raymond J. Adams

Just learning to ride a 10-speed bicycle on level ground is not the easiest thing in the world. But if you have gotten through your first lessons, you are probably starting to look at your local uphill roads. After all, one of the advantages of a 10-speed bicycle is that it enables you to ride uphill.

You may have even tried to pedal over an overpass or two. That's when you discovered that pedaling up a grade is not the same as riding over level ground. I know how you feel. The first hill I tried to pedal up rose about 12 feet over a distance of about 250 feet. I had to stop and rest three-quarters of the way up. After something like that, you wonder how you will ever be able to climb a real hill.

Watching other cyclists to see what they do is more discouraging than helpful. As beginners, we usually think that all other riders are experts. Or at least we think that they can ride better than we can, which is perhaps true. What can really bother you is the way they act as they approach the foot of a steep hill. Ninety-five percent turn around and come back. If they can't make it, how can you?

Yet it is possible to learn how to climb hills very early in your learning period. You may not immediately learn to climb them quickly, smoothly or well, but you can climb them if you know how.

But why bother? There is plenty of level ground. Why not stick to it? There is a very good reason. If you cannot handle an uphill ride, your freedom to ride where you choose is limited. Hills become walls beyond which you cannot go. Learn to master the art of uphill riding, and hills can be anything from a real challenge to just a nuisance to be ridden over on your way to more interesting things. And you are making the decisions, not the hills.

There are beginner's techniques for riding uphill. Once you learn, the improvement in your ability can be startling. The first hill I ever tried rose 200 feet over a distance of 4,000 feet, with the last 250 feet of the ride being quite steep. The first time I tried the climb, I had to stop and rest four times. I didn't care. I was jubilant. I had made it to the top. In a few days, I would be stopping three times, then twice, once, and then it would be nonstop all the way. Only it didn't work out that way. A week later, I was still stopping at exactly the same four places. I had shown no improvement whatsoever.

At the top of this hill was a side road that went up still another hill for an additional 500 feet in about one-and-a-half miles. I began climbing that one also. On each attempt, I had to stop and rest 12 to 15 times.

Another two weeks went by with no sign of improvement. Finally, in desperation, I tried a different cycling technique. To my amazement, I made it nonstop to the top of the 200-foot hill. The next day I tried both hills. I had to stop at the 200-foot mark, but I then made the 500-foot climb nonstop. The next day I went all the way nonstop. I had gone from 18 stops to none in just three days. I was totally exhausted when I got to the top, but I couldn't have cared less. I had found the secret to uphill climbing.

Before we go into the details of that secret, let's talk about your bicycle first. You need a gear that is low enough and a bicycle that is light enough. The low gear should be between 35 and 40. If the low gear ratio possible on your bicycle is much above 40, you may find those first climbs really tough.

You should try to keep the total weight of your bicycle to 36 pounds or less. Total weight here means the weight of your bicycle added to weight of a full water bottle, tire pump, saddlebag, and contents. The lighter this total weight, the easier the climb. My first climbs were made in 35 gear with a 36-pound load. When I purchased a bicycle that gave me a loaded weight of 30 pounds, I found that 38 gear was easier than the 35 had been.

This is a good time to add straps and clips to the pedals of your bicycle. Practice using them on level ground until you get accustomed to them and can make use of them. They don't make you any stronger, but they make more efficient use of the strength you have.

What had I been doing wrong? Like many beginners, I had gone out and bought books on bicycling. They all told me that I should always gear down when I came to a grade or hill. In another place in the book I had read where I should always maintain a steady cadence. Like many other beginners, I took these two rules to be unalterable truths.

Well, if you keep gearing down when you start up a hill, you are going to hit low gear sooner or later. That was what I had done. But then I made the mistake of trying to maintain my regular cadence. The obvious thing happened. The energy needed to maintain the pace I was setting was much greater than my body could produce. So I kept burning out every hundred yards.

Here is the method I used to solve the problem.

Select a hill where you have seen other cyclists riding. It is very difficult for a beginner to look at an uphill grade and know whether it is too steep or not.

Pick a hill worthy of the climb, but don't pick Mt. Everest, either. Something between a rise of 200 and 400 feet is good for a starter. You want something where you can reach the top.

If you are riding to the hill, take it easy the last mile or so. Try to be as fresh as possible when you start the climb.

Stop at the bottom of the hill for a standing-up break of a minute or less. Let your body catch its breath. But don't stop long enough to cool off. If you are starting your ride at the bottom of the hill, ride around on level ground until your warm up.

Once all of that is out of the way, you are ready to start. As soon as you start uphill, shift into the lowest gear of your bicycle. Then, begin pedaling as slowly as you possibly can without having the bicycle wobble or fall over.

You are fresh at the bottom of a hill, and most hills begin gradually. You may feel that this slow, slow pace is too easy and that you can certainly gear up or pedal faster until things get tougher. Resist that urge. No matter how you feel, hold it down as slow as you can safely move. The only time to increase cadence or gear up is when you hit a long level stretch on the way up. Even then, take it very easy. On short level stretches of 50 to 150 feet, keep the gear down and the cadence low. Use that level stretch to rest while you are still moving.

Ignore any and all riders who may zip past you on the way up. Don't try to keep up. Forget about speed, elegance, everything but your two goals. At this stage, nothing else matters. You want to get to the top of the hill and you want to try to make it nonstop.

There is nothing else that can lift your spirits like making the crest of that first hill, no matter how ragged the ride. You suddenly realize that 50 percent of the problem was mental. Just looking at a hill defeats as many riders as trying to climb it does. There is the added satisfaction of knowing that if you have just conquered a fairly difficult hill, you can conquer most other hills.

Make this climb and similar climbs a half-dozen times before you start trying to improve your riding techniques. You can start gearing up, changing cadence, or shifting up and down after you have mastered the art of just getting there. In a matter of weeks, you will find that you have nearly halved the time it took you to make that first climb.

Never forget this beginner's technique even though you go on to more sophisticated methods of uphill riding. When you come to a hill or mountain higher than you have ever attempted before, use it as you need it. You will be using it more smoothly and efficiently, of course, and combining it with other methods. I went back to much of it myself when I recently made a 7,000-foot climb that I wasn't sure I could do. If I hadn't used it part of the way, I would never have made it.

And remember, no cyclist has ever ridden to the top of a second hill or mountain until after conquering the first one.

# Downhill Riding

## Raymond J. Adams

Here are a few points to consider before taking any downhill rides.

In the beginning, *never* pedal to the top of a hill and then keep on going down the other side. Stop and take a break. Your first uphill rides can sap your strength without you realizing it. Your feeling of triumph at reaching the top of the hill can dull your judgment. As you tire, your coordination begins to diminish, just like that of a runner struggling those last 100 yards to the finish line. Stop and take stock of how you feel. Get your strength and coordination back.

Once you have learned uphill riding, there is nothing wrong with going up and down nonstop. But wait until you have more experience in judging your immediate physical condition.

Check your brakes. Don't just squeeze the levers. Check the whole system. Make sure the brake pads are secure and properly aligned.

Check the nuts or levers which hold the wheels to your bicycle. I have already seen two riders merely touch the nuts on the front axle before a long downhill, and the nuts fell off.

Never, never go above your alarm speed. As you start down and pick up speed, you are going to reach a certain point at which you feel alarm. Something in your head will tell you that's fast enough. When you get to that point, start squeezing the brakes gently to hold your speed down. Be careful about braking. Avoid the panic stop kind. Panic stop braking on level ground at 10 or 12 miles an hour may only cause your bicycle to skid (if you are lucky). The same kind of braking on a high-speed downhill run can flip you end-over-end. If you do have to brake quickly, try to lean toward the rear.

Watch out for long, straight stretches. Don't be tricked into going too fast. At the end of every straight stretch, a curve is waiting. Hitting that curve at too high a speed is as though a giant hand is trying to push you off the road making you continue in a straight line over the side.

Watch out for water on the road. You never know what is in it. It may be clear, or it may be slippery mud. Avoid trying to turn in it if you can. If the water is at a turn, slow down and take the turn easily.

Be especially careful on those tight, 180-degree turns. Slow down as much as possible.

Watch out for loose dirt, especially at the edge of the road. If you hit it at high speed while turning, it can flip the wheels of your bicycle from beneath you as easily as an oil slick.

Watch out for those shady areas with mixtures of shadow and sunlight. You are going from bright sunlight into the shadows, so it is hard to see. Those moving lights and shadows can hide amazingly large bumps and rocks.

If you wear sunglasses, get the kind with ear pieces. The pressure-stem kind slide down your nose with every bump.

If you are going downhill the same way you came up, note the hazards and remember them.

When turning left or right on a steep downhill, always keep the pedal on that side up in the 12-o'clock position. The primary reason is to keep that pedal high on turns so it doesn't scrape the curb. You shouldn't be getting that close to the curb, but in case you do, the pedal will be out of the way.

Always go down to the lower bars and get your hands close to the brakes. This is a more stable position than sitting up and working the brakes over the top. It also permits better and more precise use of the brakes.

Be sure to start off with your hands on the lower bars. Transferring down isn't as easy as you think. The faster you go, the more difficult it becomes.

# Standing Up in the Pedals

## Ray Blum

Development of good stand-up cycling techniques can advance the average biker's capability and enjoyment far more than is generally recognized. There has been a growing tendency among newer riders toward exploiting advantages in equipment, while overlooking opportunities for extending personal capability and versatility. A particularly fertile area is that of stand-up pedaling techniques.

The principal reason for standing up on the pedals is to utilize the force of gravity in applying more power, such as starting up after a stop, increasing speed or climbing hills. However, there are other uses and many side benefits.

Sally Ann Shenk

**The right technique for cycling out of the saddle. Note position of hands on the handlebar tops.**

For instance, on a long ride the change of pace and different muscles involved in getting off the saddle for a spell can provide a welcome opportunity to stretch the legs, straighten the back, breathe deeply, and ease the backside. Alternating long periods in the saddle with shorter intervals of standing up can do much to reduce fatigue, relieve monotony, and thus extend the distance that can comfortably be ridden without stopping to rest.

Pumping the pedals from a position off the saddle provides a diversified exercise and develops rhythm and balance. Wrists, arms, shoulders, and other parts of the body can be exercised in a dynamic way, while contributing to propulsion by effective positioning of body weight over the pedals on each downstroke. Leg muscles can be further strengthened in climbing hills by standing up, as is the case when pedaling smaller gear ratios from the saddle position. The long-term end result is greater climbing speed with less overall effort. Furthermore, under favorable conditions, a cyclist will actually be refreshed by a moderate stand-up climb and will be more energetically inclined toward pedaling upon returning to the saddle.

The explanation of this apparent phenomenon lies in the great boost in circulation that can be obtained. When standing, a gear ratio can be selected to provide appropriate resistance, and the cyclist's motion of transferring his or her weight alternately to each pedal can provide a controlled rhythmic contraction and relaxation of leg muscles that function very effectively to circulate the blood. The legs thus relieve the heart of a large share of the load and make it possible for the rider to operate at a higher energy output level.

Some ideas on when and how to use standing advantageously are as follows:

When starting after a stop on fairly level terrain, it is more practical and beneficial to accelerate up to speed by standing up in the cruising gear (provided the cruising gear is not too high), as opposed to going through a sequence of gear shifts in automotive style. Standing is also useful whenever it is desired to increase speed, making it practical to use a higher cruising gear by standing to accelerate or apply more power, and sitting down to maintain a steady pace on the levels.

For relief on a long ride, it is best to choose places where a brief increase of power is desirable, such as in going over a small knoll or rise. Standing helps to keep up rolling speed, avoids shifting, and at the same time provides sufficient resistance for the rider to stretch out and relax in stepping from one pedal to the other.

In climbing hills of varying grade it is also helpful to keep gear shifts to a minimum by standing and pumping harder on the steeper portions and sitting down where the slopes are more moderate.

Another point with regard to climbing is that body weight is best utilized when positioned precisely over the pedal for the power portion of the downstroke. Balance and timing are important. Experienced riders tilt the bike from side-to-side slightly in synchronization with the weight positioning motion, for the purpose of balancing the bike against the leverage of a vertical power stroke, while keeping the body's center of gravity traveling in as straight a line as possible.

The importance of developing good sitting-down pedal action is unchallenged and foremost in priority. Standing is a separate and complementary skill which can be cultivated and put to good use as described above.

Generally, the peak force on the legs when standing is much greater than the steadier pressure of pedaling from the saddle and therefore, there is more emphasis on strengthening certain leg muscles. It is significant that sit-down pedaling does not do much to develop the type of strength required for good standing ability, and therefore some practice and development is necessary.

Although cadence will be reduced while standing, rpm (revolutions per minute) should not be lowered to the point where the rider is straining, particularly when climbing hills. In those sections of the country where no hills are available, a high gear should be selected to provide the necessary resistance. However, when using high gears on the level, the idea is to relax and let your body weight do most of the work. If your speed becomes faster than you wish to pedal, shift to a higher gear. If you feel you are going too fast under the conditions at hand or have exceeded your bike riding ability, transferring some of the body weight to the handlebars will reduce acceleration while allowing you to stay out of the saddle.

As the legs gradually strengthen, and the standing technique is developed, the advantages will become increasingly apparent.

# Getting Down on Drop Handlebars

### David L. Smith, M.D.

There are plenty of cyclists, young and old, who can laugh at this. They are thin and supple and have never had any trouble folding into a horizontal position. However, there are also plenty of older, fat, stiff fellows like me who have real difficulty with dropped handlebars. For us, the bars and especially the brakes are impossibly far away. Through trial and error, I've found a few tricks that have helped me to adapt.

Move the seat forward on the seatpost (within reason). This helps to get the legs back out of the way and will tip you forward toward the handlebars. Don't forget to readjust the height and angle of the saddle.

Make sure that the balls of your feet are directly over the pedal axles, rather than in front of the axles. Moving the feet back will help to get the legs out of the way of the abdomen.

If you are in the market for a new set of pedals, the new Hi-E pedals will get your feet, and therefore your seat, about an inch closer to the ground so that you can reach the bars without bending over so far.

If you are about to buy a new bike or frame, make sure that the frame is no larger than you can safely ride. A longer head tube will allow the handlebars to ride higher. A mixte frame or a custom frame with slanted top tube will allow a longer head tube.

Change the handlebar stem for a model that can be pulled farther out of the head tube, and/or one that does not project too far forward. I use a Belleri stem on my Peugeot; I don't know if they make sizes for non-French bikes.

Use a touring-type or randonneur handlebar. Don't be afraid to experiment with brake and handlebar position and don't be ashamed of using cyclo-tourist brake levers, or safety levers, if you have to.

Give up the idea of being able to look up at the trees and sky, at least while in the down position. If you are down low enough to bring wind resistance to a minimum, it may be difficult enough to see the road ahead. Of course, when your hands are on the top of the bars, you should be able to look at the scenery.

Sunglass- or helmet-mounted mirrors are sometimes ineffective in the dropped position, as the shoulder gets in the way of the line of sight of the mirror. There are three possible solutions: use a bicycle-mounted mirror which, however, could have drawbacks by being too large, heavy, easily broken or bent if the bike falls over, and produce too much wind resistance; look back under your armpit which is easy to do for some, but not so easy for others as everything is upside down; modify the position of the head mirror upwards and outwards by mounting a piece of press-on prism on the corner of the sunglasses. This will bend the light from the mirror so that it can be seen through the sunglasses. The 15-diopter prisms are the best for this. These are available at optometry shops, usually on special order.

A piece of press-on prism can also be mounted on the top half-inch of the sunglass' lens or even on the back of the entire lens so that the distance ahead can be seen without craning one's neck so far. The disadvantage of this is that it blurs vision.

# Preventing Handlebar Palsy

## David L. Smith, M.D.

A college student had ridden a bicycle across the United States, covering about 100 miles a day. About the tenth day of the trip he noticed the onset of weakness of both hands, which became progressively worse. A medical examination at the end of his trip revealed extensive weakness and atrophy of certain muscles in the hand. The ulnar nerve was functioning poorly. The patient was forced to give up bicycle riding for several months, and even after this time the muscles were still somewhat weak.

What happened? The ulnar nerve connects with the intrinsic muscles of the hand and supplies sensation from the little-finger side of the hand. It is close to the surface at the elbow; if you have ever hit your funnybone, you know exactly what part of the hand is involved. This nerve is also susceptible to prolonged pressure or trauma as it crosses the wrist and base of the hand. Pressure, especially if the hand is in an extended position, can cause damage to the superficial branch (pins and needles, numbness) or the deep branch (hand weakness) or both, and sometimes takes months to completely reverse itself.

There are several solutions to this problem of varying degrees of practicality.

Don't ride your bicycle.

Ride your bicycle in an upright position with flat handlebars, in order to take weight off the hands.

Various changes in your bike's components might help; a shorter stem will decrease the angle of your body, thus reducing the amount of weight leaning on the bars; low-flange hubs rather than high will give a more shock-absorbing ride.

Change hand position frequently. This is the easiest solution and works in most cases. A switch to randonneur handlebars should also help as these are designed to give the rider more choice of grips.

Padding helps. You might try well-padded riding gloves or padded handlebar tape.

# Wet Weather Biking

## Thom Lieb

Cycling in the rain can be one of the most pleasurable ways to spend your time in the saddle. But unless you know how to handle your bike in the rain, wet weather cycling could cost you your life.

When your rims and brake pads become wet, even by being splashed by a passing car or passing through a lone puddle, your brakes lose as much as 95 percent of their effectiveness. You then have to grab your brake levers much harder to reach a given level of braking power.

If the road is wet, the situation is worse. During the first half hour of a rainstorm, the rain mixes with oil and grime on the road and forms a slippery solution that can cut the friction between your tires and the road to half of what it would be on a dry surface. Lower friction means lower rolling resistance, so you can ride faster than on dry roads. But lower friction also reduces your steering and braking control, causing you to skid if you brake vigorously or spill if you lean too far into a turn.

After the first half hour of a storm, most of the road grime and oil is washed away. Your traction rises to three-quarters of what it would be on a dry surface, but you still need about twice the distance to stop as you would on a dry road. At even 16 mph, you need about 65 feet to stop; coming down a hill at 50 mph, you need about 500 feet, a tenth of a mile.

At speeds above 8 mph, riding on wet roads poses another hazard—hydroplaning. The effect is caused by water being compressed under your rapidly advancing wheels. The compressed water lifts your wheels from the road surface, further decreasing your bike's traction.

Lack of brake power, hydroplaning, and lack of traction may make stopping difficult, but it is not impossible. Instead of grasping your brake levers frantically, it is better to pump them, beginning before you must stop. This braking technique removes much of the water from your rims and dries your rims through friction, cutting down your chances of skidding.

Rainy day riding demands intense concentration. Even the most conscientious rider will not be able to anticipate every potential hazard, however, and may have to occasionally stop unexpectedly. If you have to stop quickly, move your weight as far back on the bike as possible and grasp your brake levers with equal force. You may skid, but with your weight well back, there is little chance you will fly over the handlebars.

If you do skid, try to relax and remember that old rule of winter driving: steer into the skid. Panic braking will only make the situation worse, although accelerating may help. Eventually you will regain traction and control of your bike.

Before you go out into the rain, you should make sure your wheels are true and your brake pads are adjusted as close to the rims as possible. You have to put more pressure on your brakes on wet than dry days, stretching the cables and deflecting the brake bridge and arms. Unless you keep your brakes well adjusted, your brake levers may hit the handlebars before the brakes stop you.

After riding in the wet, wipe your rims and brake pads clean so your brakes will grab well the next time you go out. Do not use kerosene or other solvents which can leave the rims slippery.

There are several pieces of equipment which are particularly suited to wet weather riding. Hub brakes (coaster and disk models) work better than caliper models, since their internal parts are not affected by rain.

Aluminum rims brake better when wet than chromed-steel models. A wet aluminum rim on a wet surface requires about twice the distance to stop as a dry one on a dry surface. A chromed-steel rim, which brakes slightly better on a dry surface, requires about five times the stopping distance when the rim and road are wet.

Rims with dimpled surfaces are poor for wet weather riding. The surfaces tend to collect water, making stopping harder than with smooth-surfaced rims.

Brake pads, too, make a difference in wet weather stopping power. As a rule, long, soft pads are better than hard, short ones. Most research has shown that groove patterns in brake pads are usually ineffective for draining water and may even have a detrimental effect on braking.

Tire tread pattern also plays an important role in wet riding. Most tires have a ribbed pattern in the center, with herringbone sidewalls for good gripping on wet roads and around turns. An all-herringbone pattern has better traction on the straights, but the bee's nest pattern has the best traction of all in wet or dry weather. Matte and smooth treads are slippery when wet.

The best equipment and technique mean little if you cannot be seen in the rain. Bad weather makes it harder for you to see motorists and, more importantly, harder for them to see you. Lights are highly recommended, as is bright clothing. Yellow is the most visible color in bad weather.

Since rain is usually accompanied by wind, you will want to wear clothes which fit closely to minimize wind resistance. If the weather is cool, you will also want to remain dry to conserve body heat to stave off cold muscles and hypothermia. Wool clothing is fine for light rains, keeping you warm even when it is wet. For heavier downpours, the various Gore-Tex parkas, pants and chaps will keep you dry from the elements and from yourself by letting your perspiration escape.

Once you become hooked on wet weather riding, you might want to invest in a set of mudguards or fenders. These keep you dry and keep road dirt from being thrown onto you, into your eyes and into the faces of anyone riding less than 50 feet behind you.

# Bike Handling in the Pack

## Owen Mulholland

The best way to become a good bike handler is to ride with others. Even on a modestly paced ride one must constantly adjust one's pace to that of the others. Every rider in a group must be sensitive to all companions' maneuvers, the variations in route and the strength and direction of the wind. It can be hard at first. Either you're working like mad to close a gap or hitting the brakes to avoid ramming the rider in front.

Eventually, it all becomes second nature. You can chat comfortably with your friends, and still keep in close formation with the riders just in front, notice and avoid that chuckhole, move over slightly to give clearance to a possible opening door on a parked car, stand up to kick over a little hill, change gears without changing tempo, and perform the myriad necessary tasks a competent rider must do to make riding smooth and trouble-free.

Unconsciously, your level of sensitivity becomes very acute. Like a herd of pedaling radar scanners, a group of riders is constantly checking a host of possible influences, screening them for importance, and reacting well in advance to negate any difficulties.

Take a group of six racing down a road. Up ahead is a parked car. The silhouette of a person in the driver's seat is visible. Everyone in the group notices it. Without a word they all move over a couple of feet to the left to avoid the possibility of hitting the car door should the occupant open it. An observer watching the whole scene might merely see a bunch of riders out for some fun and never guess at the marvelous sensitivities and planning necessary to make that fun ride just that.

This is bike handling at its simplest. Turns, fluctuations in speed, traffic, hills, attacks by other riders, and so on, make even more demands on one's ability to perceive, analyze and act instantaneously.

In a race, especially a criterium, there are a number of sharp corners that must be negotiated with the least loss of speed possible. Ideally, of course, the fastest line through a corner is that which most closely approximates a straight line from the outside of the turn, across the apex at the inside and to the outside again. Then consider the compromising factors. Sewer grates, bumps, sand, oil, water, anywhere along the ideal line can render that line useless. Take a bunch of riders and throw them all into that corner at once, and the fastest line becomes something altogether different. The apex becomes the slowest part of the bunch, and riders looking to move up the field have to go around the outside.

I have emphasized the brainwork necessary for racing because I consider it to be the foremost requirement. Yet the body must be able to translate the necessities of any situation into physical inflections

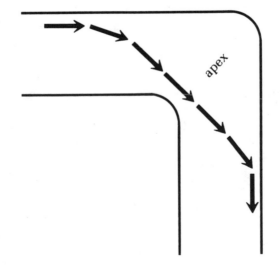

**The ideal pedaling line through a corner.**

that will meet those necessities. Swooping into a turn by yourself, you should move to the outside as you make the approach. (This will be near the center line for a right-hand turn on a road open to traffic.) A gentle yet firm stab at the brakes at the last moment, with the emphasis being on the rear brake as you begin to lean into the turn, accompanied by a slight shift of the body back on the saddle and a drooping of the right shoulder and, possibly, an outward pointing of the inside knee, and you're set to take the turn at maximum speed. Stay loose. Don't let little undulations upset your attitude. Keep the inside pedal up, and only start to pedal again after coming out of the turn when you are sure you have adequate clearance.

More factors confuse the picture when doing this in a group. Corners are the critical factor in criteriums. The rider in front can start pedaling before the rider behind, so the rider behind must accelerate sharply to make up the gap. Most criteriums have at least four corners per lap around roughly a one-mile circuit, which must be covered at least 25 times. So at a minimum there are commonly 100 corners in a criterium, each requiring a jump. This is much more taxing than a steady, fast pace, and anything that can ease those jumps is obviously to the benefit of the rider. One technique is to use shorter length cranks to permit earlier pedaling coming out of a turn. If you can begin pedaling at the same time as the rider in front of you, there won't be that gap to close. Another method is to take a slightly wider line, which will allow some overlapping of the leading rider's rear wheel. While the rider in front is accelerating hard out of the turn, you can accelerate more leisurely and slip into that slipstream at your discretion.

Mountain turns are roughly similar to criterium turns in terms of technique. The big difference is that such roads are often unfamiliar to the bulk of the field, so it is necessary to read the corner before entering it. Once you are set up and committed to a certain line in a turn, there is very little latitude for correcting. You can only lean over so far, and any braking done in this position is a very touchy matter. Many turns are very deceiving. The decreasing-radius type is the most vicious. They keep getting tighter and tighter, sometimes coming around 200 degrees. Anyone who sets up for a 90-degree turn and finds him/herself a few seconds later in the midst of a seemingly endless circle can be in for a lot of trouble. It's always wise to keep a bit in hand for the unforeseen.

If possible, look below when entering a mountain curve. If you can see the road exiting the turn, you can pretty well guess its dimensions. Lefthand hairpins that give a full view of the oncoming lane lend themselves to utilizing the full width of the road if no traffic is coming. Two fingers on each brake are enough. In a straight line you can use a terrific amount of pressure on the front wheel. Due to the weight transfer forward, any severe braking on the rear wheel will make it lock up and skid. Once you enter the turn, you can still do some braking, but it has to be rather gentle, with the emphasis on the rear brake. Gravel and large bumps can change all this, of course. At all times you must have an idea of who is around you and where. You should be able to surmise from a quick look over your shoulder while entering a bend if a rider behind is setting up to come by you. Through the turn you must hold your line as far as practicable. Sudden deviations can bring down others who are counting on you to remain steady.

Just as much as cornering, pace line work requires total concentration. You must simultaneously keep an eye on the wheel just in front as well as the riders farther ahead. Unless the wind is coming from straight in front or behind, echeloning will be called for. Once you've done your bit at the front, you should make a sharp move into the wind. This is the signal for the next rider to come through as you start to slide to the back. Stay close to the other riders to get whatever shelter is available and tuck in behind the last rider the moment your front wheel clears his/her rear wheel. This is the most vulnerable moment, since you have to accelerate a bit back up to the pace of the others at your weakest moment. Care and concentration can minimize the risks of getting dropped needlessly.

Gear shifting can properly be considered part of bike handling. The finer derailleurs are quite precise when utilized properly. Like everything else, it's a matter of anticipation. You should already be in the right gear to respond to the attack. Having to shift before countering can waste precious moments. It should never be necessary to look at your shift lever to find it. Habit should be your guide. Shifting should be done in a firm, fast manner.

Occasionally, it is necessary to jump the bike into the air to miss an unavoidable hill or bad railroad crossing. It's not hard if you pull up evenly with the legs and arms. Belgian pros can even jump their bikes sideways over curbs, out of the cobbled streets onto the smoother bike paths. If you see an obstacle and must jump it, accelerate if possible. The faster you're going, the more distance you can cover in the air.

Standing still is at the opposite end of the speed continuum. It is a common technique in track sprinting and occasionally useful at the beginning of a road event to permit a fast takeoff. You need a slope to balance against. Stand up out of the saddle and turn the wheel up the grade. Keep pressure on the downslope-side pedal to counter the tendency to roll down the hill. Once you balance these two forces, you will be standing still on two wheels.

T. L. Gettings

**The peleton in a road race. Cyclists position themselves to get maximum wind protection.**

These, then, are some of the common techniques required for good bike handling in races. All it takes is practice, practice and more practice.

# Developing Road Rapport

## Josh Lehman

I bicycled into New York City to visit a friend several years ago. He was amazed that I had threaded the bike through traffic. "How do you ride that in New York?" he demanded.

"Carefully," I wisecracked. Then I explained my tactics in terms a fellow New Yorker could understand. I compared bicycling with basketball. "The trick is to 'key' on the action, just like on the court. When you're bicycling the city streets, everything is in motion. Some movements, like an opening car door or an opponent moving to the hoop, are crucial right then. Other moves should be stored for future reference, like the patterns which bus drivers or the other team weave.

"I try to pick up on all the cues and clues I need, so if the need arises, I'm prepared to make a good, quick judgment and the right move. That means periscoping around a busy intersection by catching reflections in the store windows. It also means tracing that taxi which is tailing me, seeing with my ears if it's turning or continuing in my direction.

"As a city cyclist, you're part of a team sport. The only problem, though, is that often the other players don't realize you're on the court."

On your long tour, the confusion of the city may be left far behind. Yet you must still ride that fine line between reverie and reason no matter where your wheels may spin. You need what I call "road rapport"; some riders refer to it as the sixth sense.

Cultivating your intuitive bicycling skills is a basic touring requirement, complementing riding strength, a fine-tuned machine, and well-honed touring gear. Being prepared for the full range of situations affords a greater degree of safety, security and enjoyment. But that doesn't preclude spontaneity, by any means. Though the potential for serious injury cannot be ignored, that realization shouldn't immobilize you.

Being aware and being prepared allow you to enjoy your tour because you have more confidence. Instead of dreading danger, you

Sally Ann Shenk

**A cyclist should position himself on the roadway so that he's plainly visible to motorists.**

learn how to recognize it, how to avoid it, and how to respond in a crisis, as need be.

Since most road information is visual, your eyes provide much of that sixth sense I mentioned. I was lucky enough to inherit good eyesight, so glasses aren't part of my normal wardrobe. But whenever I tour, sunglasses are on the top of my packing list and almost always protect my eyes as I ride. They not only glareproof my eyes, but provide a shield against flying insects. (If you've ever had a gnat plastered on your eye while riding, you know how painful it can be.)

Glasses also provide a point of attachment for a rearview mirror about the size of a dentist's mirror. If you have tried wearing one clipped to your helmet and found it difficult to keep in adjustment, try mounting it onto your glasses. You will probably find it easier.

Other options include handlebar-mounted mirrors and those worn on your hand or wrist. If you have never used a mirror, give it a chance. It may be a good complement to your other senses—an easy way to maintain a check on the road behind you. Remember, though, it doesn't negate the necessity of turning your head for a backward look before a maneuver like changing lanes.

What about seeing in darkness and rain? My rule of thumb is that if it's dark and wet, I ought to be thinking about getting off the bike and off the road. There are occasions, however, when touring after sunset or before the sun comes up is a real treat. Then I am ready with good lighting, reflective tape, reflectors, and light-colored clothing.

There are also times when riding in the rain is required or, believe it or not, sheer delight. Other precautions may be in order. Also, don't forget those cotton cycling caps, prime examples of lightweight form and function, with brims designed to shield your eyes from strong sun as well as stinging rain.

Even though most cues are visual, hearing also makes an important contribution to your sense of the road. Often you will hear something before you see it—that barking dog running toward the road, that truck about to round the bend. And, while your eyes can't see in all directions at once, your ears can. So learn to listen. Sometimes it's your ears that tell you where your eyes should look next. Attentive listeners quickly develop a familiarity for the usual sounds of the road. You should also, if you haven't already, learn the sound of your bike and your touring gear. Then if you hear something peculiar, you'll know to investigate.

In addition to sharpening vision and hearing, it's crucial to develop your sense of the relationship between other vehicles on the road and your bike. Here's an exercise in relative road speed for your next group ride. In the exercise you will gradually speed up enough to catch a rider ahead of you on the road. Begin by selecting the rider. Then, using all the clues you have at hand—topography, wind, and other road references—try to calculate at just what point you'll pass that cyclist. Accelerate, and when you have caught up, see how close you came to your prediction.

Now project yourself into a typical highway situation. A truck is coming up from the rear, and a car is approaching in the opposite lane. What you will need to do next depends on numerous variables: your position on the road relative to those other vehicles, the width and surface of the roadway lanes, the presence of a shoulder and its condition. Will these two vehicles pass each other at the same time they pass you? If so, what will you need to do about it? Perhaps nothing if it's a wide roadway; maybe speed up or slow down to allow that semi to come around you after or before meeting the approaching car. Maybe you'll want to situate yourself in the lane and signal the trucker to slow down and wait to pass.

If you sense that your defensive bicycling bag of tricks has been depleted, you may just have to ride off the road. I've never been forced to do that, but I'm always prepared for the possibility. If a smooth, paved shoulder lies flush with your traffic lane, consider yourself lucky. If not, be ready for the conditions you might encounter and to respond accordingly. You should visualize the variables: the type of shoulder surface—grass, gravel, sand, mud; shoulder width; what borders it—a ditch, a guardrail, a flowered field.

Of course, you want to make your transition from the road to its border as smoothly as possible. Try to act without panicking, so that you don't avoid one hazard by creating another. Even so, under some circumstances, leaving the road may mean that a spill is inevitable. If you must do so—perhaps to avoid some vehicle which otherwise would hit you—generally your best course is to exit a wide enough angle so that you can't fall back onto the road.

To practice on your next ride, start looking around. Now pretend that at that instant you must ride off the road. Will the transition be bumpy or smooth? Quick or gradual? A shock or a matter of habit?

Look up the road and think ahead. Next to that tall tree just around the bend, a bale of hay is blocking your lane; a car has stopped in the opposite lane. There is no time to brake to a halt; you must ride off the road.

Or imagine this. All of a sudden your partner's pannier opens and that evening's fruit salad, apples and oranges, bounces all over the road. Rather than risk a tumble, you opt for the shoulder.

Should you actually practice riding off the road? Some riders will feel that preparing mentally is sufficient. Others have actually practiced the maneuver under the safest conditions they could find and recommend that other cyclists do likewise. If you follow that course, use caution and be sure to wear your helmet.

Whatever methods you use to achieve it, road rapport is an important aspect of your development as a cyclist. Cary Peterson, an accomplished racer on the U.S. Women's National Team, has described what we're talking about: "Riding in a tight, fast racing pack, you must be alert to any variation—a rut in the road, sharp slivers of glass, or another rider straying or slowing ever so slightly. But a good pack will ride and glide around the obstruction like a school of fish around a reef; cleanly, smoothly, instinctively." So will a skilled bicycle tourist react to any unusual situations. Familiarity, it is said, breeds contempt, but on a bicycle, familiarity breeds safety and assurance.

Certain touring paraphernalia may seem odd at first, but soon you'll feel naked without it. Just as my helmet has become a habit, so my bikes don't leave the house without a bell. Some locales require a bicycle horn, bell or other "audible warning device," but my logic transcends legalities. Bells make your presence known to those unsuspecting bicyclists whom you were about to slip silently by, to that distracted pedestrian about to step off the curb into your path, or to the car driver who failed to scan the rearview mirror and is now opening the door in your way.

A loud clear chime permits you to say "Hey, here I am!" but not menacingly. This is central to road rapport. If you're skeptical, ride along with a bicyclist who has a bell. Before long you'll know how indispensable they can be. Whether used to serenade starlings, to bark back at dogs, or to avert an accident, the bicycle bell is a humble yet mighty mechanical servant.

On the other hand, remember that just as cyclists often may not be seen, sometimes they will not be heard, even with a bell. Don't let your bell (or whistle, if you prefer) lull you away from defensive cycling techniques when you need them. Be ready to brake or dodge as you must.

Therein lies the crux of road rapport, this sixth sense of cycling—the ability to anticipate, to avoid, and when necessary, to act. The Bikecentennial safety report summarizes the situation appropriately: "Bicycle touring is as safe as cyclists make it. *All* roads, even the most carefully thought-out bike routes, have traffic and other hazards. One must *always* ride with caution."

In his lyric and probing discourse on sports, *The Ultimate Athlete* (New York: Viking, 1975), George Leonard often alludes to the Zen archer, the athlete who epitomizes this calm state of preparedness. Bicyclists about to set off on that long tour, or around the block, would do well to note the archer's stance: "Expect nothing. Be ready for everything."

# Avoiding Wheel Accidents

### David Gordon Wilson

Accidents which result from the locking of the front wheel are extremely dangerous and often result in severe injuries and paralysis. In what follows I analyze accidents of this type which have come to my attention, sometimes painfully, and suggest steps which should be taken by all bicyclists to avoid this potentially disastrous occurrence.

## Consequences of Front Wheel-Locking

When something occurs at speeds of above two or three miles per hour to cause the front wheel almost instantaneously to stop rotating, inertia carries the rider plus machine in a circle around the front wheel. From low speeds, impact will be a short distance in front of the front wheel, usually with the head. The hands are often trapped on the handlebars and cannot be used to lessen the severity of the fall. From higher speeds, contact with the ground will be at a greater distance in front of the point of wheel-locking, and the rotation of the rider may result in the spine of the rider taking the full force of the impact.

An accident resulting from front wheel-locking is likely, therefore, to be extremely dangerous with consequences that are often tragic.

We can take simple precautions to minimize the likelihood that front wheel-locking will occur. The precautions are sometimes obvious, particularly when one is sensitized to the possibility of the occurrence of the accident. Some less obvious precautions are mentioned below.

# Causes of Front Wheel-Locking .

**Trapping of Bags and Clothing:** Some people carry shopping or book bags slung from the handlebars, and some drape spare clothing, perhaps a raincoat, over the bars. These frequently become entangled with the front wheel. Usually the wheel rotates several times before jamming completely, so that the resulting accidents, while extremely dangerous, are not quite as catastrophic as some of the following listed.

**Luggage Falling into Spokes from Front Luggage Carrier:** A young man had a wrench tied to a carrier over the front wheel. Vibrations displaced the wrench which fell into the front wheel and jammed across the forks. He was catapulted over the hood of a car. This may be one of the few cases where impact with a car saved more serious injury.

The use of a front carrier is extremely dangerous unless the carrier is equipped with a securely fastened bag, box or basket from which nothing can be shaken out to contact the wheel. An empty bag must not itself be able to droop over the carrier in such a way that it, or its straps and buckles, can contact the wheel.

**Generator:** A young woman bought a new generator and mounted it on the front fork in the trailing position. The next day she was riding over a potholed street at very slow speed. The generator was shaken into the spokes causing immediate wheel-locking, and her face was smashed against the rough pavement. Because of the slow speed she merely suffered a mild concussion and facial lacerations.

Preferably generators should be located on the rear wheel.

However, if there are major advantages to installing the generator on the front wheel, then it should be in the forward position where wheel rotation will take it away from the fork rather than into it.

**Brakes:** If a caliper brake becomes detached it can fall into the spokes and cause almost instantaneous locking of the wheel. One man on an almost-new 10-speed bicycle became paralyzed from the neck down after breaking his spine from a fall caused by his front brake becoming detached.

The front brake bolt and nut should be checked frequently. At least one and preferably two locking nuts should be used. A lock-washer alone is not sufficient. As an added precaution, the brake cable can be tied to the frame so that, should the bolt come loose or fracture, the brake will not fall into the wheel.

**Fenders (mudguards):** A man bought his wife a 5-speed, sports bicycle at a department store, unassembled. He took it to a local automobile shop for assembly. He and his wife went out for their first leisurely ride. After two or three miles, the front wheel suddenly locked, and the woman was thrown over the handlebars, severely injuring her face and breaking her jaw and some teeth. She was bicycling at little more than walking speed when the jamming occurred.

Subsequent examination of the bicycle revealed that the person who assembled the bike had either forgotten to put on the nut securing the fender to the fork crown, or had put it on too loosely. The fender then fell onto the front wheel, where it probably rubbed for a while and then was carried forward by the wheel rotation. The lower fender stays were attached to brazed-on lugs on the front fork so that the stays were shorter than the wheel radius. The stays were composed of a single loop of steel wire of about 5/32-inch diameter. As the fender was carried forward by the wheel, this loop rapidly tightened onto the tire, squashed it flat and then collapsed the rim inward, eventually putting a V-notch into the rim.

At some time in the life of a bicycle, steel fenders are certain to rust, aluminum fenders will corrode, and plastic fenders will become brittle. Therefore, while it is vitally necessary that the fender nuts be tight and be of the self-locking variety, these precautions alone will not prevent a serious accident should the fender break or should a twig become caught in the spokes and force the fender stays around, buckling the fender and tightening the loop stays onto the wheel.

These loop stays should be banned, preferably by agreement among bicycle manufacturers, or, if not, by government regulation. The type of fender used on lightweight bicycles, which incorporate adjustable slip joints that give way in the circumstance of the above

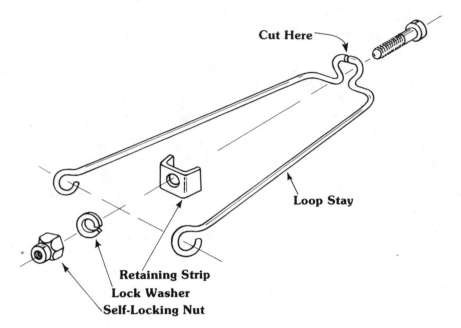

**Safety improvements to fender loop stays.**

accident, are much safer. If you have a bicycle with the wire-loop stays, I recommend a modification similar to that shown in the illustration.

**Spoke Reflectors:**  Some spoke reflectors are short enough to twist around on a single spoke and either become bridged across the forks or across the fender stays, causing the type of accident mentioned above. The spoke reflectors should be either too short or too long for this type of rotation and bridging to occur.

**Wheel Dropping Out:**  An M.I.T. graduate student bicycling along a typical Boston-area potholed road, saw a large chuckhole ahead and jerked up on his handlebars to lift the front wheel over the depression. Unfortunately, the wheel nuts were not tight, the wheel fell out, and he went forward until the fork ends hit the road. He suffered serious injuries.

New bicycles made to conform with the Consumer Products Safety Commission's standards (CPSC) must incorporate means to prevent the front wheel dropping out even if the nuts are loose. However, many existing bikes do not incorporate any such provisions. With the increasingly popular practice of removing the front wheel to lock it together with the back wheel to a parking meter when leaving the bicycle, there are obviously increased dangers of forgetting to tighten the front wheel spindle when reassembling the bike for the onward journey.

You can make this occurrence less likely in a bicycle without the CPSC required provisions by squeezing the fork ends together somewhat so that they have to be sprung apart to insert the wheel.

**Front Fork Failure:**  Many years ago, at the top of a steep hill near the English-Welsh border, I was chatting with a local bicyclist when I noticed that one blade of his fork was completely severed and the other had a crack in it. I pleaded with him not to ride his bike until he had a new fork, particularly not to go down the other side of the hill. He did not seem concerned about the danger of the probable accident because he had fallen off before. But people who live through a fast wheel-locking accident know that it is more than a mere fall.

Several years ago, I had two different contacts within 24 hours with people telling me of riders who had broken their skulls while riding Moulton bicycles. In each case the fork had snapped off just above the fork crown. I found out that for the first nine months of the production of the Moulton bicycle, the forks had been made by an outside contractor, who had put in a very sharp radius at the point where the fork tube was brazed into the crown, and the resulting high stress caused the fatigue failure. Moulton had recalled all the bikes whose owners could be reached but could not cover those taken abroad. I'm sorry to say that when I wrote to another bicycling journal to ask that Moulton owners be warned, the letter was not published. Let me repeat the warning here: anyone who is riding a Moulton with a serial number of K.64.29 or lower and which has not had the front fork replaced is sitting on a ticking bomb.

Front fork failures are not strictly front wheel-locking incidents, but the results are equally or more devastating.

**Wheel-warping:**  A round, true, tension-spoked wheel is really in a state of unstable equilibrium. The stable state is something nearer a figure-eight. Wheels with too few spokes or with contiguous spokes missing, slender rims, rim damage, or when bearing too heavy a load, sometimes spontaneously try to adopt the figure-eight state and lock in the forks. I have had this happen twice to the rear wheel but not to the front wheel. The remedies are to avoid these conditions.

Commuting and recreational cycling are so beneficial to the individual and to society that they should be made as safe as possible. Awareness of the dangers will lead riders to take simple precautions to lessen these dangers.

# Riding with Traffic

## John Schubert

Thousands of people would still be alive today if only they had bicycled on the right side of the road. Wrong-way cycling is more than illegal and stupid—it's a leading cause of bicycle deaths and injuries. And yet so many people do it anyway.

Wrong-way cycling has the appearance of safety to those people. They think, wrongly, that they can see hazards better than cyclists who ride with traffic. This grave mistake, legitimized by daily habit, has been cited by many transportation experts as the single biggest obstacle to a more healthy bicycle-automobile traffic mix in this country.

"It's just madness for bicyclists to ride facing traffic," said Kenneth D. Cross of Anacapa Sciences. "I see little hope that motorists can be taught to scan the left shoulder for wrong-way cyclists."

Cross, author of one of the world's most thorough studies* of bicycle/motor-vehicle collisions, found wrong-way cycling a factor in 17 percent of the 919 accidents studied. And another excellent study,[†] authored by Allan F. Williams, found wrong-way cycling in 15 percent of the 861 accidents studied. Moreover, Williams found wrong-way cycling a cause of 25 percent of the accidents among cyclists over age 14—old enough to know better.

In both studies, wrong-way cycling was far and away the biggest single accident cause.

These findings are not supported by accident statistics from Europe. That's not because wrong-way cycling is safe there (or anywhere), though. Europeans, who are much more familiar with the bicycle than Americans, know better than to ride on the wrong side. It's not tolerated by European police. Police in the United States should be so concerned. In Boulder, Colorado, an active program for enforcing traffic regulations for cyclists met with such scorn and indifference among patrol officers that the police depart-

---

*A Study of Bicycle/Motor-Vehicle Accidents: Identification of Problem Types and Countermeasure Approaches—Volume I, Kenneth D. Cross and Gary Fisher, Anacapa Sciences, Inc., Santa Barbara, CA 93102, 1977.

[†]Study done for the Insurance Institute for Highway Safety in December, 1974.

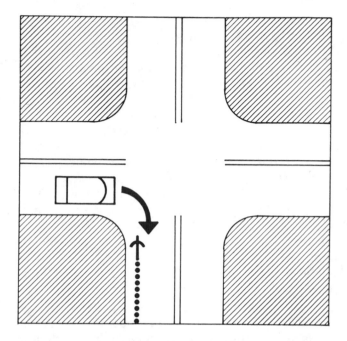

One of the most frequent accident types which results from wrong-way riding occurs when a motorist makes a right turn toward the wrong-way cyclist. The motorist usually looks only to the left before executing the turn, and in these accidents often collides with the cyclist before even seeing him/her. This is only one of many wrong-way riding accidents which can occur at intersections. To see how wrong-way riding complicates intersection traffic patterns, just ask yourself how this cyclist could possibly make a safe right turn.

ment found it necessary to give each officer a quota of bicycle violations to fill. And in many other United States cities, where no such quota system exists, police treat cyclists with not-so-benign neglect.

Despite the grim accident reports and the international example, one can still find people purporting to teach bicycle safety by insisting that their students "ride facing traffic." And, worse yet, those people can still find books and brochures which inculcate wrong-way riding with all the authority of the written word. The persons who wrote these deadly books are somehow oblivious to the knowledge that laws in all 50 states require all cyclists to ride on the right.

The motivation for wrong-way riding begins with the widely held belief that a car, any car at any time, is a threat to the cyclist's safety. Combine this with the fear of the unseen, and the wrong-way cyclist has ample motive for not riding where unseen cars are in a position to (the cyclist fears) hit him or her.

But the whole purpose of traffic laws is to allow road users to rely on the predictability of each other's movements. The cyclist who fears that all cars approaching from behind are likely to be injurious must learn three things:

Participation in traffic demands that the cyclist obey the laws which keep traffic orderly, and that he/she allow and expect other traffic to do likewise.

The laws protect the cyclist most fully when he/she is on the right side of the road.

Riding on the left upsets the orderly pattern. The cyclist is exposed to many more hazards which he/she can't see or hope to avoid.

What are those hazards? Why is the left shoulder inherently dangerous?

The bicycle is a vehicle. This has both legal and practical implications.

"There has been a lot of misinformation on this issue," said John English, director of research for the National Committee on Uniform Traffic Laws and Ordinances and a well-known authority on bicycles and traffic law. "I suspect this is because people believe the bicycle is like a pedestrian, and they know the pedestrian is supposed to be on the left—but they're wrong. Vehicles in this country ride on the right, and the bicycle is a vehicle."

The bicycle shares most attributes of other vehicles (such as automobiles). It goes fairly quickly, can only turn a corner so tightly, needs smooth pavement underneath to function and requires considerable distance to stop; more distance than a car requires at the same speed.

Because of these limitations, the bicycle cannot magically dance out of the way of trouble. If it tries, it may fall right in the path of oncoming traffic. It must follow a path which is least likely to bring it into trouble.

The wrong-way cyclist forces all road users to deal with a hazard coming from a new and unexpected direction.

"The motorist does not expect the bicyclist to be coming from that direction," English said. "Ask any driver education teacher where he teaches people to scan."

Vince Durago, creator of the well-known *Sprocketman*, a bicycle safety pamphlet published by the North Carolina Department of Transportation in Raleigh, North Carolina, puts it another way:

"The vast majority of bicycle accidents occur because the bicycle's movements are unpredictable," Durago said. "Motorists are getting tricked by wrong-way bicyclists who virturally force them to run them over."

The wrong-way cyclist can do nothing right when he/she reaches an intersection.

There are no rules or legitimate paths for a wrong-way cyclist to follow at an intersection. The cyclist must create an *ad hoc* path to get through the other vehicles' paths. The cyclist can't see motor vehicles with which he/she is on a collision course—such as cars coming from behind to turn left or cars making a right turn towards the cyclist. And those cars can't see the cyclist either.

Any path a wrong-way cyclist picks through an intersection is, by definition, on a collision course with a motorist who had no reason to expect a hazard coming from that direction. When a motorist finally does see a wrong-way cyclist, it may take the motorist a fatal minute to realize in which direction the cyclist is heading.

Should the wrong-way cyclist have to veer out into the roadway, he/she is in much greater trouble than a right-side cyclist.

Frequently occurring hazards such as broken glass, potholes, pavement seams, or a disappearing shoulder force a cyclist, no matter which direction he/she rides in, to veer toward the center of the road. When on the left, the cyclist is on a collision course with the next oncoming car, with a closing speed equal to the sum of the bicycle's speed and the car's speed.

Using the modest figures of 15 and 25 mph for the bicycle and car respectively, the wrong-way cyclist approaches the car head-on at 40 mph or 20 yards per second. If the cyclist rides on the right, the closing speed is only 10 mph (5 yards per second). Moreover, since kinetic energy varies with the square of the speed, the wrong-way cyclist's potential impact is 16 times as severe as the right-side cyclist's impact. It's the same as the difference between falling from a 2-story building and falling from a 30-story building.

The wrong-way cyclist is forced to cross paths with the oncoming car at a moment of neither's choosing.

The motorist overtaking a right-side cyclist can follow and wait for a safe moment to pass, whereas the motorist approaching a wrong-way cyclist must cross paths right then, however dangerous a moment that might be.

If the motorist is faced with approaching traffic, especially if he/she faces an oncoming wide load or a car struggling to complete a passing maneuver, the motorist may be forced to veer toward the wrong-way cyclist to avoid the oncoming traffic. To add insult to injury, the greater overtaking speed and opposing directions of the wrong-way cyclist demand greater lateral clearance for safe passage.

Wrong-way cyclists frequently collide with pedestrians and with right-side cyclists.

These accidents often result in broken bones and hospital stays for innocent parties.

Yes, cyclists are sometimes struck from behind when they ride on the proper side of the road, but data from Cross's study tells us this accident type is no excuse for wrong-way cycling. Some 70 percent of those accidents are on narrow rural roads after dark, and one-third of the time the motorist is intoxicated.

Cross found that more than half the victims had "rear lighting equipment that met the current lighting standards," but he is one of many researchers who believes these standards are pitifully inadequate. Victims of these accidents were usually very hard to see.

And there's no guarantee that the accident wouldn't occur if the cyclist were facing the other way. Remember, the cyclist usually has no shoulder to ride on and is nearly invisible to the motorist.

There's no question that riding on the right side requires maturity, judgment, careful attention, and steady nerves on the cyclist's part. It takes practice for a cyclist to become used to the proper role in the traffic mix. But with this practice, the cyclist will learn that motorists who pass on the left are, by training and instinct, ready to allow for and safely pass slow-moving vehicles in their paths. The chances of those motorists hitting the cyclist are quite small—unless the cyclist breaks the rules.

# The Right Clothes

## Raymond J. Adams

People ride bicycles for many reasons. It's one way of expressing ourselves as individuals apart from our work, family or community. It's a side trip off the beaten path of our daily routine.

Yet, when it comes to clothing, most good cyclists all seem to wear the same things. There are good reasons for this contradiction. If you are a beginning cyclist, you may not be sure of the how and why of it. Here, in general, are some of the reasons why cyclists wear what they do.

Not all cyclists need the same kind of clothing. Your choice may depend on how often, how far and how long you ride. I ride in a nearby park after work. One of the riders I see regularly is a middle-aged gentleman who is invariably wearing tennis shoes, khaki pants, a dress shirt and a cowboy hat. Considering the distance he rides and the sedate speed at which he travels, his outfit is probably appropriate to his needs.

## Shoes

If you are just starting to ride, shoes are not a critical item. But there are a few things you must consider. Always wear shoes that have shoestrings. The slip-on type shoes are usually too loose. Shoestrings permit you to fit the shoe snugly to your foot and avoid chafing. They also save the shoes from wear.

Many cyclists will tell you that tennis shoes should not be used for riding because the soles aren't thick enough, and your feet will soon start hurting. However, if you are a short distance rider or you are just beginning to ride, tennis shoes are quite sufficient. They are relatively cheap and easy to buy. They can be used like any other shoes when not riding.

Avoid extra thick soles on any shoes that you use. You will want to feel the pedals in the same way you want to feel the gas pedal or brakes on your car.

If you are at the stage where you want to take longer rides of more than 10 or 15 miles, you should consider getting regular riding shoes. This is especially true if you have straps and clips on the pedals. Riding shoes will take the wear and tear you will subject them to, they slide easily in and out of the straps, and the soles are strong enough to protect your feet. After you have used toe straps and riding shoes for awhile, try riding once again with tennis shoes. You will be surprised at how big and bulky they seem.

If you buy riding shoes, don't attach shoe cleats to the soles unless you are specifically interested in racing. If you have to ride through city traffic, there are too many stops to make cleats practical. And you can't walk around in them.

Don't buy the ultra-light riding shoe meant exclusively for racing. Get a shoe that is also intended for walking. This way you have shoes strong enough to permit you to use them to go shopping, wander around at a bicycle meet or stroll around a park. My present riding shoes are only now beginning to show any real signs of wear after approximately 6,500 miles of riding and at least 20 to 30 miles of walking.

## Pants

Anyone who is going through their first riding lessons should wear long pants which are reasonably thick and strong. Khakis or blue jeans are fine. There are a lot of reasons why long pants do not make good riding clothes; but for the beginner, there is one overriding reason why they do. Wear them for protection. You will probably fall more times in the first 500 miles you ride than you will in the next 5,000. It is a lot better to tear up a pair of pants than to do the same to yourself. On your early rides you will also spend a lot of time banging your shins on the pedals when you try to start or stop. Long pants ease the pain somewhat and reduce the size of the bruises.

Don't wear your favorite pants. Sooner or later you are going to rub them against the chain. You will never get the grease stains out.

If you never go beyond riding around the neighborhood, long pants may be the only kind you will ever need. But as soon as you begin riding as far as five or ten miles at a time, it will become obvious that they have serious drawbacks. They are much too heavy. Perspiration will add to their weight. In addition, they stick to your legs above the knees when they get damp. At every turn of the pedals, you have to break them loose, and they slide damply up and down your legs.

Short pants are lighter, but they still stick to your legs above the knees and still rub against them. Very short pants solve these two problems, but create a new one. They ride up, and after a few miles you feel like you are sitting on pieces of rope. Pants with slightly longer legs than track pants offer a good compromise. Many riders use them and never try anything else.

If you are really going to ride regularly and seriously, you should sooner or later consider regular riding pants. Unlike other pants, they fit snugly around your legs. They don't move against the legs as you pedal; they move with them.

In addition, the crotch is lined with a soft chamois to prevent chafing, so they are worn without any undershorts. For the first few rides this feels awkward, and you have nightmares about what will happen if they split, but you soon forget all about it in a week or two. The chamois does have one shortcoming. After a half-dozen washings, all the natural oils are gone, and it becomes as stiff and rough as sandpaper. Use a moisturizer such as Noxzema or baking soda to soften it up. If you use Noxzema, put it on the day *before* you ride. Noxzema always feel cold, and putting the pants on immediately after you have rubbed it into the chamois can be a real eye-opening experience.

As soon as you begin wearing riding shorts, you will realize that you need a riding shirt. Until now, almost any lightweight pullover shirt would do. But regular shorts may not have pockets, and the average shirt does not have enough pockets. Cycling shirts come with a variety of pocket combinations. A good one for your first purchase has three pockets across the back near the bottom and two in front by the collar. Five pockets give you enough space to carry all you will need.

Use the front pockets for such items as car keys or your wallet. Since you are leaning forward as you ride, they don't rub against you. Use the rear pockets for handkerchiefs and snacks. Unless you are style conscious, buy the least expensive shirts which are usually cotton.

# Gloves

Gloves are one of those items that you don't need at first unless your hands are unusually tender or you want to protect them should you fall. Even if your hands are sore after the first times you ride, give them a chance to toughen up a bit before you rush out and buy a pair of gloves.

When you begin taking longer rides, you are probably going to reach a point where your hands need some protection. Just where that point is varies with the individual. In my own case, I found that I could ride up to four hours without gloves. Anything beyond that and my hands began to look and feel like raw hamburger.

Almost all wear of riding gloves is in the palms. So the fingertips are cut off and the back of the glove is open knit. You might want a second pair of gloves for winter riding. Try the regular mountain climber's leather gloves with the wool inserts. Be sure to buy a pair that will take a beating.

# Sunglasses

A beginning rider should always wear sunglasses or goggles of some sort when riding. It is difficult even for an experienced rider to keep from falling or wobbling into traffic when something gets in the eyes. And if you ride after work as I do, you will be running into clouds of gnats during the late afternoon. There will be larger insects to contend with on country roads. During this past summer, I have had everything from bumblebees to grasshoppers slam into my eyeglasses.

If you do use sunglasses, get light-tinted ones or two pairs so you have something to use on cloudy days or late afternoon rides at dusk. Buy a pair with safety lenses. You might even get shields for the sides. Since I began using the side shields, I have gone through clouds of insects so thick I had to stop and pick them from my nose, lips, ears and hair. But I have never gotten one in my eyes.

Avoid glasses with the pressure stems. Get the kind where the stem wraps around your ears or has a strap that goes around your head. Glasses with pressure stems start sliding down your nose with every bump, particularly on a downhill ride.

# Techniques for Touring

## David C. Barudin

I was surprised to find out that skilled cyclists expend only 40 percent of the energy on a tour that new riders do—and have ten times the endurance. (I thought everybody worked as hard as I did!) How's it done? Basically, it involves using all your biking muscles—legs, arms, back—together in rhythm. It's something like saving wear on a truck by braking and down-shifting at the same time.

In terms of bike and rider, this means a smooth and complete leg motion; consistent cadence; shifting gears without losing either one. It also means using arms and other muscles to help pull up a hill.

There are three basic points to developing these skills. First is to practice riding your bike. That's right; not an all-out Olympic program, but persistently. Using your bike for regular exercise and recreation makes touring a lot easier.

Give yourself time to ride every week, as much as possible. This entails a degree of discipline. My discipline is not awfully vigorous. (But it's fine for me.) I bike a lot around town and jog a mile a day. I also do yoga, the best thing there is for bicycling. Come Saturday, I can ride 60 or 70 miles and feel good. You may need to discipline yourself to a greater degree at first.

The second point is learning efficiency. It comes from riding a lot. If you've ever ridden yourself to a standstill on the first day of a tour, the tired-out second day teaches you about efficiency. The tiredness and strain on your muscles, ligaments and joints are from overtaxing yourself. I always have to be cautious to keep my pace down that first exhilarating day, or I'd do myself in. An efficient touring pace is a moderate, steady tempo; a smooth rhythm that you can pedal with for an hour or more and still recover a normal, untired feeling during a short break.

The third, and most important, point in touring is knowing a little about how your body operates when you ride, so you can work along with it.

If you're aware of your body's vital signs, then you know and can feel why bike touring demands a moderate, steady cadence. It's efficient and healthy because of how it affects your blood flow. Steady cadence contracts leg muscles in rhythm with your heart rate, squeezing blood back to your heart. This makes blood flow easier and your heart work less. As your breathing falls into the rhythm, working muscles get bathed in plenty of oxygen-rich blood. Pulse and blood pressure should go up a little, but at a steady rate. If these vital signs aren't right, then slow down or make your cadence smoother.

If you're an older rider or someone who doesn't exercise regularly, you'll want to be cautious of vital signs—heart rate, pulse, breathing—when you begin riding. Build up slowly. You'll be pushing the strongest riders soon enough.

Begin with a modest cadence, about equal to or just above your heart rate—70 or 75 rpm or less. Ride in medium gears and on level roads. Your pulse shouldn't throb or drastically increase. If it does, slow down.

At first, ride for 15 or 20 minutes, then get off and rest. Check how long it takes your heart and breathing to get back to normal. As you work into shape, you'll recover more quickly. Then move up your initial cadence, use higher gears and put some small hills into your regular ride.

Conditioning comes naturally on a bike, so ride for fun. Lower gears feel easy, but they do a lot for you. Make efficiency a goal and practice smooth leg motion, steady cadence and changing gears.

# Normal Aches and Pains

Of course, you can expect soreness from riding, but you won't experience serious strains if you ease into it and ride often. The normal aches and pains are a nuisance but are not cause for alarm.

**Stiff Neck, Shoulders and Upper Back:** You'll feel this especially if you ride with drop handlebars. You can relax this ache as you ride. Sit tall with your head up. Throw your shoulders back and touch the back of your neck, one hand at a time. Work your way down your back, counting as many vertebrae as you can reach. This stretching feels great. Also practice arching your back for a straighter ride posture; a lot of bicyclists ride very hunched over.

**Sore Leg Muscles:** The quadriceps muscles and ligaments in the upper leg are the workhorses in pedaling. These large thigh muscles can become very tender on a long, hilly tour. Calf muscles actually do little work and may not bother you at all.

A moderate, smooth cadence and using arms and shoulders during upgrades are real muscle-savers. As you exert yourself during a climb, breathe deeply so the large quadriceps get enough oxygen. Deep, full breaths exhale useless carbon dioxide and water vapor and bring in plenty of fresh air. It also helps to take short, periodic breaks. I like to ride for about an hour, then rest 10 minutes.

**Side Pains:**  I get these once in a while after lunch. Sometimes they extend into the chest area. To shake them, I've always had to climb down and walk a short distance. They're impossible to ride with!

**Tired Seat:**  I don't think there's much relief for this. As much as bike seats are oiled, bottoms still hurt. Not until after my second summer tour did riding become relatively painless. So take heart that maybe your next trip won't be as hard.

**Stiff Wrists, Numb Fingers and Hands:**  Wrists can get awfully stiff, especially over rough roads. Riding gloves help. You can also get cushioning and traction by temporarily deflating your tires about five pounds when riding over rough and gravelled surfaces. Padded handlebar tape helps. It's available commercially, or you can devise your own.

For numb fingers keep a loose but firm hold on the handlebars and shift your grip often. When you stop to rest, rub your hands briskly. Then wring and shake them out like a wet towel. Good touring handlebars are designed to give you several possible hand positions and thus ease the strain.

Check to see that the bike is adjusted correctly for you. As a general rule, set the seat so your legs are just about fully extended on the bottom pedal. Tighten handlebars slightly below the level of the seat. Then slide the seat forward or back for comfort.

You can save yourself a lot of minor aches and pains by simply limbering up before you ride. Bikers seldom do this. But your body will work much better if you warm up for the work ahead. Take just five minutes and gently flex and stretch all your muscles. You'll feel looser and ride more comfortably.

Sudden temperature changes, such as letting yourself cool off too rapidly after pedaling hard, aren't healthy. Repeated heat buildup and loss weakens your resistance to fatigue, and you tire easily. Little summer breezes can cool you off quickly, so carry a shirt or light sweater and slip it on when you stop—you'll cool off slower and more evenly. Tuck it away after you're warmed on the next leg of your tour. You'll be a lot fresher later in the day when you need that extra push.

Bike touring, especially in summer, isn't the time to knock yourself out in a rubber or plastic workout suit. The increased sweating doesn't produce permanent weight loss; it's gained right back. What it does is prevent sweat from evaporating and keeps body temperature high. This makes you a likely candidate for heatstroke, heat exhaustion or worse. All you need do to stay trim and fit is ride a lot.

Sally Ann Shenk

After a blind turn, these cyclists ride the shoulder for a short while. Note the potential for rocks in the road.

When you stop to rest, don't just throw yourself in the shade, swearing you'll never get up again. Instead (and this is a much better way to treat yourself), slip on your shirt or sweater and take a short walk. Carry your water bottle and sip it slowly; breathe deeply. When you lie down, choose a slight incline and point your toes down. This gets blood to them readily.

When you're ready to push on, walk your bike first. Don't get right on. This walk tells your system it's time to go and reminds your legs of what they're there for; or that they're there!

Getting back on your bike; this can be a very awkward situation, especially if you're carrying gear. A lot of cyclists spill on the gravel shoulder or the lip of the pavement. Walk your bike onto the road and get on out there, even if you have to wait for a break in traffic.

## Taking Hills

Hills and headwinds are the real tests in biking. Both mean work. No technique will flatten out muscle-stretching roller coasters or three or four miles of steady grade or an awaiting mountain. But smart riding can make hill climbing easier and make you stronger as the day goes on.

Moderate and steady rhythm is the key. Rhythm in hills becomes a full-body rhythm using as many muscles as possible. A slow, crawling pace or full-steam-ahead only drains your energy reserves. Think in terms of the overall ride. Bikers have traversed the highest Rocky Mountain passes by conserving strength to last the whole trip. So find a cadence that fits your energy and stick to it. Don't push extra hard to make the climb go faster.

Approach a hill with a little speed. Get a good bite into it before gearing down. Gear down as you feel pressure building, before you have to. Take deep and full breaths as you work for the top. I think you'll find that legs and wind get stronger cycling if you use these techniques in up and down terrain.

Rest frequently, especially in mountains. Resting, eating and drinking in regular, small amounts is part of meting out your energy. Just stop and enjoy where you are. Your own work got you there! Stretch your legs and nibble high energy, nutritional snacks. Have your sweater handy for rest stops and the breezy ride down.

When you're coasting down snaking mountain roads, use your brakes. You broke your back on the way up, there's no advantage in taking a chance on the descent. Remember, patches of sand and gravel accumulate at horseshoe turns and switchbacks.

## Touring in a Group

Most people enjoy bike touring as a leisurely ride in the country with others. It's a nice way to spend time with friends, or make new ones.

Group touring should let everyone go at his/her own pace without anyone getting lost or separated. That takes preparation and compromise.

In groups that I've toured with, there are always a few who clip right along and others (like us) who sometimes dally. I often stop to photograph and write in my notepad, even if it means climbing off for a better look at something.

Your group should decide how much structure it needs. If it's small, each rider should know the people ahead and behind. And those with repair knowledge should take turns at the rear. What makes touring fun is helpfulness. So be on the alert for the problems of others, especially new riders.

For short, weekend tours our groups have printed tour routes for each rider. Meeting places are clearly marked. These are stops for mid-morning, lunch and afternoon breaks, and no one goes on until everyone has caught up. Faster riders can double back and ride with someone, explore off the route or just relax and wait. If a rider hasn't arrived in due time, someone goes back to hunt them up. On longer trips riders should have an emergency phone number they can call if they get lost. This can save a lot of time and hunting.

Have the next leg and meeting place straight before taking off again. That means going over all the turns on the map before starting out. If a turn is tricky, the first rider leaves a marker. (An arrow sticker or colored handkerchief works well.) The last rider has to remember to retrieve the handkerchief. The tour should end in plenty of time to set up camp and look for stragglers.

# Efficient Touring

## Russell Davis and Jim Pickering

"Bit 'n' bit" is a British term. Basically, bit 'n' bit is a group of two or more riders traveling in close single file, with each rider taking a turn (a bit) at the front. With efficient use of this tactic, riders can cover a given distance in much less time than if each individual were to travel by him/herself. As experienced cyclists know, the basis of this efficiency involves the fact that the cyclist at the front of a group does more work than the people riding close behind. The differences in work load (as much as 25 percent or more) are due to the windbreaking effort accomplished by the lead rider. When people ride individually, as in time trials, each person must be his/her own wind breaker. When riding in a group, this is done by the leader and all the others in the group can rest and ride out of the wind. The bit 'n' bit system takes advantage of this by sharing the work among all members of the group. Each person works hard for awhile, and then, after relinquishing the lead, can take a well deserved rest at the rear. This gets the most out of all members of a group of riders and is also an excellent method of training. It works best with experienced riders who are all of comparable ability.

Bit 'n' bit involves certain risks which are not present in individual riding, since one misjudgment by one individual can bring down every rider in the group. The risks decrease in direct proportion to the experience of the riders and to their understanding of the precautionary rules of the game. Consequently, it is important that each person who plans to participate in bit 'n' bit touring be aware of the rules. Unfortunately, these rules are unwritten, and there is no convenient means by which a rider can learn the fundamentals of bit 'n' bit cycling without joining in and trying it. Lack of formalization, variation of these rules from place to place and a not uncommon attitude of "don't worry—we'll just play it by ear" all complicate the problem.

As a solution, we have attempted to formalize the techniques and customs of bit 'n' bit touring. These have been developed by the touring Tucson Wheelmen, and have been found to be appropriate to conditions in southern Arizona. They are presented in the hope of providing a suitable indoctrination for beginners, and also in the expectation that they may sharpen the techniques of all who participate in this exciting and rewarding form of cycling.

The bit 'n' bit group should form single file along the right edge of the road. The first rider is temporary leader. The position of the leader's bike will determine the position of the rest of the riders in relation to the edge of the road. The first rider should maintain about three feet of clearance between his/her bike and the right edge of the road. This distance must vary depending upon the type of road; a very narrow road might require a position closer to the edge (because of traffic), while gravel and debris on the shoulder might require moving toward the center.

The second rider in line should choose a position so that the front wheel of the bicycle is about one to three feet behind the leader's rear wheel, and offset from about six inches to one foot either to the right or left. Other riders in the line follow the same procedure as the second rider, except that the direction of offset is no longer optional. If the rider directly in front is offset to the left, then the following rider must offset to the right . . . and so forth on down the line.

Never brake suddenly (except, of course, in an extreme emergency).

Never move abruptly out of the line without first announcing your intention of doing so. Unexpected and unannounced jumps are both dangerous and discourteous.

As much as possible, maintain a steady pace and steer a straight line.

It is necessary to stay on the brakes constantly. This can be tiring, but it is simply one of the costs of bit 'n' bit riding. The only rider in the line who can relax is the leader, and he/she must pay for this privilege with the work required in breaking wind.

In case of an emergency (especially involving potential collisions among members of the group), each rider should escape in the direction of the offset. However, riders who are offset left must always be aware of the possibility of traffic approaching from the rear.

It is the temporary leader's responsibility to avoid road hazards and to announce them to the other riders in the line. The leader should yell "glass" or "hole" or "tracks." If the leader must apply the brakes, he/she yells "brakes" before doing so. These calls are then passed back by the other riders so everyone in the line is alerted.

As a matter of honor, and for purposes of maximum efficiency, the temporary leader should do a fair share of hard work at the front. Depending on the pace, wind and grade, for strong and highly trained riders this might be a period of time as long as several minutes. For riders who are less strong, a fair share might be as little as 10 or 15 turns of the crank. The point is: when it becomes your turn to lead, you must stay in front long enough to do your share, but for only as long as is reasonable for your level of conditioning. It is important that you do not stay in the lead beyond your capacity. If you stay in front too long, you'll eventually be dropped, and then the entire bit 'n' bit team will have to work harder because you are no longer available to share the work. Occasionally, the time may come when a rider must drop out. This occurs only when there is a big difference in the ability of the rider who is dropped as compared to the other riders in the group. The dropped rider should feel no loss of honor; he/she has benefited by the training experience gained while staying with the group, and they have benefited by having him/her in the team.

In most cases, the pace which is selected by the group should be based on the speed that can be handled by the weakest rider. As in all team efforts, it is important for the better riders to protect those who are not as strong. Dropped riders suggest inefficient teamwork, although sometimes this can't be avoided.

The leader should first move slightly to the left and then glance over the left shoulder to check for cars. If there are cars approaching from the rear, he/she should move back into the original position. This must be repeated until the traffic is clear.

If there are no cars approaching from the rear, the leader should glance once more over the left shoulder (a final check) and then move the bike to the left and out of the line of riders. He/she should move to the left only enough so as not to interfere with the other riders. At this point, the second rider in the line is now leader.

The ex-leader should then decrease speed just slightly so that the line of riders slowly moves ahead. As the last rider in the line approaches, the ex-leader must accelerate to match his/her speed to that of the line. At the right moment, the ex-leader must "take" the rear wheel of the last rider.

The point at which the ex-leader positions him/herself behind the rear wheel of the rear rider is critical. If he/she has slowed down excessively, there may suddenly be a gap which develops between his/her bike and the riders ahead. If fatigue level is high, this may result in being dropped. A distance of as little as six feet is sufficient to cause a complete loss of the drag effect, and without this there is no rest for the weary. Even in cases where a weary ex-leader is able to make up those lost six feet, the effort may be just enough to prevent being able to maintain the pace long enough to recover.

It is important that the new leader, who is rested and eager, does not charge ahead and accelerate the pace. In general, the first responsibility is to maintain the pace, not to increase it. There are exceptions, of course. If the last leader stayed too long or misjudged the pace and allowed his/her speed to slow to below proper pace, then it is the new leader's job to pick things up. However, this must be done carefully and gradually, and there should be no speed increase until the ex-leader is properly positioned at the rear. If the last leader has increased the pace excessively, it's the duty of the new leader to slow things down. Remember, this is a team effort. The object is to get from one point to another as efficiently and rapidly as possible.

Bit 'n' bit is a rewarding experience. The esprit de corps, the rhythm, the pace and the training benefits are all part of the enjoyment.

# Places Not to Ride

### Raymond J. Adams

Most cycling advice stresses some positive aspect of riding. It tells you what you should do in order to enjoy your trip. I would like to do the same thing, but with a different approach. I would like to point out times and places when and where you should *not* ride. Some of the problems I will bring up will seem obvious. Unfortunately, most of them are the kind that become obvious only after we get caught in them.

This blind spot we all have occurs for two reasons. In the first place, it is easy to get all worked up about a coming ride. You start looking forward to it so much that you never get down to thinking about the details. And even the details we think about are optimistic ones. We like to think about what will go right instead of about what can go wrong. Riders also get into trouble because they don't always plan a ride. They merely prepare for it. Here's what I mean.

Let's say you feel you have learned the basics of cycling. You are getting pretty tired of just circling around in your own neighborhood. You want to strike out on some 10- to 15-mile rides of your own. So you start reading bicycling books and magazines. You learn how to tune up your bicycle before a ride, what tools and equipment to take, how to pace yourself, which gears to use, what kinds of food to bring along, when to eat it, and so on.

All of this is solid information, and you will be in trouble if you do not have it. But this is merely the preparation, getting ready to ride. What about the route itself? Where are you going to ride? Planning a route involves a lot more than just tracing lines on a map. What do those lines really represent?

There are four things you have to consider every time you take a longer ride. They never show up on maps, and three of them are invisible. These are temperature, humidity, wind and rain.

I live in the Los Angeles area. Before I began riding, I spent a good deal of my life going from an air-conditioned house to an air-conditioned office in an air-conditioned car. Oh sure, I knew when it was hot or windy; or so I thought. But when I began cycling, I was amazed (and embarrassed) by how little I really knew about the local weather. I didn't have to learn the local weather all over again. I had never really known it.

Take a close, hard look at the temperature and humidity in your area. You may not be as familiar with them as you think. Every time I have had to limp home has been because I underestimated one or the other.

A couple from Phoenix planning a July bicycle tour of the Bayou country in southern Louisiana may think the trip will be easy because the temperatures in Louisiana are lower than in Phoenix. It may not be. Humidity in Phoenix in July averages 28 percent. In New Orleans it is a soggy 66 percent, and there is an average of 15 days of rain in July—usually not long rains, just brief showers. But a Louisiana summer shower can drench you in 30 seconds—if the humidity hasn't already done so.

Wind is something most of us know little about until we begin cycling. Who cares which way the wind is blowing when you are in a car or at the beach? Yet few other things can ruin a ride so quickly. The places to watch for wind are beach areas, mountain passes, canyons, the bottoms of hills or mountains, and wide-open flat country.

You may be surprised to discover, as I did, that wind patterns are reasonably dependable. They may change from morning to afternoon, or with the seasons. But once you learn them, you can usually predict them on an average day.

I am not saying you should always avoid windy routes. A ride with a brisk wind at your back is wild. You feel as if you are ready for the Tour de France. And it does good things to your ego when you find that you can use that 105-inch gear without killing yourself.

Learn them all—temperature, humidity, wind and rain patterns. If you don't, a discouraging percentage of your rides will turn out to be failures.

There are also places you should plan to avoid, or at least ride with extreme caution. You might schedule your visits for the off-season. Be careful when riding in popular national parks or vacation spots. Scenically, they may be the best places to ride. But they have their hazards. The roads are usually narrow and the traffic is heavy. Worst of all, too many motorists are pulling wide trailers they can't handle or carrying oversized campers on underpowered trucks they can't drive over roads they are not familiar with. Watch out for those side-mounted rearview mirrors motorists stick on their cars to help them see behind the trailers. No matter how many times you have driven to such an area, remember that driving through it and cycling through are two different things. If you plan such rides, get in a lot of practice on progressively more difficult and traffic-laden streets.

When most of us plan a somewhat longer ride, we usually plan it a couple of weeks ahead of time. Never just pick a date and let it go at that. Check to make sure that nothing involving a lot of people is taking place on your route the day you plan to ride. Such events as rock concerts, sporting events and county fairs can clog a road for miles.

If you are riding to a specific place such as an amusement park, make sure it will be open. A lot of them close one or two days a week. And don't arrive at 8:30 A.M., only to find out the place does not open until 10:30.

Be wary of bicycle paths near beaches or heavily populated areas if you plan to ride on the weekend. Some of the riders have not been on a bicycle in months. I have had more close shaves in two hours on such a bicycle path than I have had in two months on the road.

Another route to avoid when planning a ride is one along streets lined with what I call "one-story businesses." This kind of street is usually found in large cities and can stretch for miles. It usually consists of a dull and endless string of plumbing shops, stationery stores, florists, gas stations, liquor stores and hamburger stands. And there is a traffic signal on every corner. The traffic is bad, the streets are usually littered and the scenery is lousy.

Pay close attention to the road surface you are going to ride on. That hard, glossy blacktop road you drove over in December can turn to sticky glue in July. Avoid dirt and gravel roads unless they are hard-packed. Stay away from old roads that haven't been fixed in years. When you get home, all you will remember is that you have spent the day dodging a few thousand chuckholes.

Try to avoid heading west into the late afternoon sunset. The sun in your eyes can be quite uncomfortable. But that is not the main reason. That setting sun is also right in the eyes of drivers coming up behind you.

Never time a long ride so closely that you expect to arrive home just before dark. Too many things can go wrong. I have gotten to the point where I can arrive at home within 30 minutes of my estimated time, no matter how long the ride—if nothing goes wrong. Since there are some things you just can't anticipate, always have that time cushion. On a ride I took last September and which I will never forget, I had five flats in 10 miles. Who could anticipate that?

Don't depend completely on bicycle touring books when riding through an unfamiliar area. All too often they forget to tell you about that small connecting road between two parts of the route. Don't place too much trust in such books that are four or five years old. I did that two summers ago. I took a 40-mile circular trip that was described as a "delightful ride along tree shaded lanes through the quiet countryside." But times and the quiet countryside had changed. The last half of the ride was a traffic-clogged nightmare of new housing tracts, hamburger stands and gas stations. If you do use such routes, bring along the relevant pages of a detailed city atlas. Maybe you can find an alternate route home.

Always take a close look at the map when planning a trip on some quiet country road. It may be as quiet as you had hoped. On the other hand, it may be the only through route for miles around, or the main road from the city to a nearby vacation spot, and the traffic will drive you out of your mind. When you pick a side road, make sure it is really just that.

Watch out for circular routes with no shortcuts home. I am one of those riders who hates to take the same route out and the same route back. I love circular or loop rides. But unless you are reasonably sure of your capabilities, don't go off on such a ride through the countryside where the road that you are on is the only one around. Halfway through you may find that you have overextended yourself, or it is hotter than you expected, or there are more hills than the map showed. A direct route home could save your day. '

Rolling hills can be a problem. They can often be more difficult to ride over than one giant hill. On a big hill, you can at least turn around and coast back. It's those hills where there are 100- and 200-foot hills, one after another, that can trap you. Each hill looks easy by itself. What happens if there are 20 such hills on the route and you burn out after the first 10? You are trapped either way.

So always be wary of the negative aspects of a trip when planning a ride. Eliminate all you can before you start. You will find a lot of others on your own.

# Beyond Safety

## Raymond J. Adams

If you are a cyclist who rides in city traffic, there are some safety practices you should consider.

First of all, there are occasions where you have to fight your own reflexes. Let's say that you are moving downhill on a medium grade. You hear a truck coming behind you and cars are coming uphill. There is a curb on the right. Suddenly you see that the road ahead is littered with glass. You are going too fast to stop in time.

This is the moment to fight that instinctive reflex that would make you try to avoid the most immediate and visible danger. Veer right and you will hit the curb. Veer left and the truck will hit you. If you must sacrifice something, then let it be the bicycle tires. Hold your breath and go through the glass. More often than not, you will make it without a flat. But if something has to be flattened, better the tires than you.

Recently a friend and I were coasting down a steep road in a nearby park. He was ahead of me. As he went around a sharp corner, he saw where water sprinklers were really showering the road. On a reflex impulse, he veered left and lost control. Fortunately there was no traffic, but he did run into the opposite curb.

It would have been so much easier to ride through the water. But it was a situation he had never thought of. When he had to face it for the first time, there was no time to think it out. He simply reacted.

Try to decide now, ahead of time, what you would do in these and similar situations. At a time of crisis there is no time to weigh alternative courses of actions. Talk to other cyclists and find out what kind of problems they've run into, and get their advice.

Bridges, for example, have all kinds of hazards for the cyclist. The first thing to remember is that they are almost always much narrower than the road you are on. There is no small lane on the right for you to use.

There are short bridges and long ones. Let's take the short ones first. When you come to a short bridge (200 feet or less), stop and look behind you. If traffic is light, wait for an opening and ride across quickly. If you can't find a break in traffic, walk your bicycle across on the pedestrian walk.

If you do ride across, there are three common hazards to watch cut for. Many bridges have an expansion joint at both ends. This slotted joint is extremely hard to spot from any distance. Running into one of them is the same as hitting a grating. Many bridges also have small drainage slots along the side all the way across. Some have small, ½-inch-high markers glued to the roadbed at the end of the bridge to guide vehicular traffic. Many of these markers are half hidden in gravel and sand.

I used to ride over long bridges, but it got to be so nerve-racking that I now walk. And even if it happens to be legal where you live, it isn't a good idea to try to ride on the pedestrian walkway.

I tried it once. It was on a bridge in the country. There were no sidewalks or houses on either side, and I hadn't seen a pedestrian in 20 miles. After a couple hundred feet of riding, I looked over the side. The dry riverbed was over 60 feet below. The railing was only 3 feet high. I was riding less than 2 feet from it. I quickly got off my bicycle.

Short tunnels in most cities are usually well lighted and generally offer no real problems. Tunnels in the countryside are almost never lighted and have all kinds of problems.

Most of them are in mountainous country where motorists don't expect to find cyclists. And very often the motorist doesn't see what is not expected to be there. If the tunnel is short, you can often ride through. Don't forget to remove your sunglasses or you will be practically blind. Such rides can be nerve-racking under any circumstances because you usually cannot see bumps, cracks or debris.

Nearly every tunnel has a sidewalk, even though many are never used for weeks at a time. An experienced rider can usually ride on the sidewalk. But if you lack experience, walk. The curved ceiling often seems to be pressing in on you in the gloom. It's very easy for this illusion to force you over the curb onto the road. And I have never been through one of these tunnels where the sidewalk was not littered with glass and debris thrown out of passing cars.

Normally, the proper place to ride is on the right side of the road. There are certain occasions, however, when it is wiser to take up a full lane. This happened to me when I turned onto a main street.

It was an older, narrow street. It had a parking lane, but every spot was occupied and the traffic was very heavy. I was practically brushing the parked cars, and those that were moving were almost doing the same to me. If I deviated from my course two or three inches, something was going to hit me, or I was going to hit it. I didn't dare try to stop. It was too close for that.

At the first break in traffic, I pulled over into the middle of the car lane where I could be seen easily but not passed—and I stayed there. I rode as fast as I could to show drivers that I wasn't there just to bug them. I got off that death trap at the next intersection.

That unhappy experience turned suddenly into a good one. The street that ran parallel to the crowded one was empty. I rode for miles in peace and quiet, one block away from the traffic.

Never go on sightseeing trips on busy streets. Walk if you want to do that. A couple of years ago I decided to take a sightseeing trip down Hollywood Boulevard for a while and then switch over to Sunset. I didn't see a thing on the trip. The traffic was so heavy I spent all of my time and attention just staying out of trouble.

Everyone tells you to watch out for gratings. Forget the unwritten rule about gratings being found only at intersections by the curb. You will find them in the middle of the block, the middle of the street, at intersections, in driveways, alleys and parking lots.

Try to develop the same sort of mental system about gratings that most of us have about red lights when driving a car. If you are driving along and the light turns red at the next corner, an alarm goes off in your head to call attention to it. Try to do the same thing with gratings—learn to see them the instant you enter a block.

Most bicycle safety books tell you always to ride on streets that have parking lanes. Anyone who rides knows that this is not always possible. Nearly all streets bottleneck now and then. Many hilly roads that are the only route through an area do not have parking lanes. Few country roads do.

There are many ways you can deal with this problem, but there are at least three exercises you can practice.

For city riding, practice riding as close as you can to the curb without hitting it with the pedals. Ride slowly the first few times and practice only where there is no traffic. You may have to do it when there is.

Learn to ride in a straight line. The first time you try this, use the long, straight lines on the surface of a large parking lot. Get out there early when the lot is empty. Next, look for a quiet country road. Many of these have a white line along the edge of the road to warn cars that the edge is near. Practice following the white line where there is no traffic. Move to the right of it when you hear something coming up behind you.

Then move over to the right and practice riding between the edge of the road and the white line. See how long you can stay there. You will learn two things. Since this is the very edge of the road, the strip available to you may quickly narrow from two feet to a couple of inches and then widen again. This is where you really learn accuracy in steering. You also learn how to ride over bumps and ruts. It's a lot better to learn these things at your own pace than to have to learn them when a giant truck is thundering up behind you.

Accept the fact that if you are just learning to ride in city traffic, there are times when the wisest thing to do is stop. Don't try to bull your way through every situation and hope for the best.

Let's say you are riding along in the parking lane. A car is parked up ahead. As you begin to move around it, you hear heavy traffic behind you. Moving out and inserting your bicycle in that narrow slot between a parked car and moving traffic is more difficult than it seems. If you have any doubts, stop! Let the traffic pass and then move out.

If you are just learning to ride on city streets, you may have trouble looking behind you. Every time I tried it at first, I nearly fell off my bicycle. Or worse yet, I wobbled out into the street. There is a way around this problem.

Get yourself a rearview mirror and attach it to the left handlebar. Rearview mirrors have disadvantages. If you carry your bicycle inside your car or station wagon, it is always in the way. You can't adjust the mirror until you begin riding. (I adjust mine in the parking lot.) And that mirror sticking out can be a hazard if you fall and land on it.

In my own case, I simply felt it was better to suffer these problems than to risk falling off or wobbling into traffic. But make your own decision.

If you install a mirror, use it to look behind you whenever you hear traffic. But constantly practice looking over your shoulder when the mirror tells you the road is clear. Learn to see at least a block behind you. Then get rid of the mirror. Never let it become a crutch.

These are only a few of the techniques you can use to minimize risks while riding. There are many others. Try to learn as many as you can before you ever need them. A trip isn't a good one unless you make it home.

# Stem Extension—
# Key to Comfortable Riding

### David Weems

If you needed a new stem for your bike, what features would you check first on the new one? Its finish? The kind of expander plug? What about a recessed-allen-head adjusting bolt, would that catch your eye? Or would you give highest priority to the extension length of the new stem?

The desire to own a good-looking bike is a healthy one, but the only characteristic mentioned above that significantly affects how a bicycle feels while you are riding it is the last one, stem length. Many riders overlook the importance of correct stem length, or, even worse, choose a stem length by appearance alone.

I first learned the importance of getting the right stem length a few years ago when I bought an expensive new 10-speed. It was fine for short runs or showing off in a crowd, but after a few miles of riding I could feel the strain of an overextended riding position in my neck muscles and the tingle in my hands. I went to a bike shop and asked to see their stock of stems. The fellow behind the counter showed me a half-dozen models, all at least as long as the one on my bike. I told him I was looking for a stem with a shorter extension.

"That's odd, all of our customers want longer ones," he said.

I suspect that if he worked in a shoe store and I asked for my usual size, 10½D, he might say something like, "But most people are buying 9s this year."

Any bicycle manufacturer that has been in business for many years will have a good idea of the right stem extension for the typical rider on any given frame size. But you may not have a typical arm/torso/leg length ratio, or your riding habits may require a different stem. How can you check your stem length to see if it is just right? There is an old rule of thumb—in this case, a rule of fingertip. Put your elbow against the front end of the saddle and extend your arm toward the stem with fingers extended. The fingertips should reach the flat section of your handlebar where it passes through the stem. This measurement gives a rough estimate of the right stem length.

Fred DeLong, in *DeLong's Guide to Bicycles & Bicycling: The Art & Science* (Radnor, Pa.: Chilton, 1978), suggests another way. Sit on the saddle with one hand on the top of the bar, the other arm hanging loosely at your side. Then swing your naturally bent loose arm forward so that your hand falls on the bar. DeLong says that you can determine from this exercise whether the bar is extended properly or not. This is probably a better method than the elbow and finger method, but it has a catch to it. DeLong undoubtedly has a precise feel, from long experience, of just the right body angle to assume while making the test. A novice might sit too upright, or bend too far forward, for comfortable riding.

You can make minor corrections in reach by moving the saddle forward or backward. Some riders try to compensate for the wrong stem length this way, but it usually doesn't work. If the bicycle was built along racing lines it undoubtedly has a long stem extension and a saddle already set farther forward than would be typical for a touring bike. Instead of correcting for a bad stem, you should use the saddle adjustments to test various saddle to handlebar distances, then get a stem that will let you put the saddle near the middle of its adjustment range. Try each setting on a ride that lasts at least an hour, enough time to show an uncomfortable posture. You'll find that a change of even a fraction of an inch can make a difference, especially if you plan to use your bike for touring.

If your bicycle has flat handlebars, the chances are that the stem has a shorter than desirable extension. English 3-speed bikes have a typical stem extension of 1¼ inches, not enough for many riders. The most cost-effective mechanical change you can make on one of these bikes is to get a stem with a greater extension. The difference in handling for riders with long torsos or arms is amazing. Before you make the change, set the saddle so its nose is at least 2½ inches or

David B. Weems

**Dropped bars, 4½-inch stem extension, 23-inch frame. For this rider the position would be suitable for racing, but uncomfortable on long tours.**

David B. Weems

**Dropped bars, 3-inch stem extension, 23-inch frame. This bike gave a feeling of relaxation, indicating less strain. Note difference in the angle of the back in the two shots.**

David B. Weems

Flat bars, 1¼-inch stem extension, 23-inch frame. The knees got in the way on turns and back position was too upright for comfort.

David B. Weems

Flat bars, 2½-inch stem extension, 22-inch frame. Much more relaxed and comfortable than the bike with the 1¼-inch stem extension, even though frame is a bit small. Rider is compensating for smaller frame by moving hands forward on grips. A better performance could have been obtained with a 23-inch frame and, say, a 3-inch stem extension.

more behind a vertical line that passes through the center of the crank spindle. Then estimate the proper stem length by assuming a comfortable, slightly forward posture and applying DeLong's test.

Another change you can make on a bike with flat bars is to rotate the bars to get the optimum hand grip angle. Most riders with flat bars have to bend their wrists excessively to grasp the bar because the hand grips are horizontal or, even worse, tilted upward. By tilting the bar so that the ends point toward the ground you can often make a significant improvement in your riding position without investing a penny in parts.

The photos on pages 74 and 75 show three bikes with 23-inch frames and one with a 22-inch frame, but different stem extension lengths, ridden by the same rider. One of the bicycles is called a "24-inch" frame because Schwinn uses a slightly different method of measuring their frames than other manufacturers. Of the two bikes with dropped bars, one required too much reach for this middle-aged rider. After changing to the bike with 1½ inches shorter stem extension, I immediately could sense a feeling of relaxation that, to me, indicated less strain.

The bikes with the flat bars produced the opposite effect. When I changed from the bike with the typical short stem extension of English bikes with flat bars to a smaller English bike with a 2½-inch stem extension, the improvement was striking. Even though the second bike was slightly too small for me, I found that my knees no longer got in the way of my elbows. And with my body inclined slightly forward, the jolt to my spine from rough roads was much less noticeable. In fact, after experimenting with the longer stem I found that I could make the flat bar bike as comfortable, at least for short trips of an hour or so, as a dropped bar bike. Its only disadvantage was the single hand position.

A younger rider with the same body measurements might prefer the dropped bar bike with the longer stem extension. His back would make a more acute angle with the ground, a posture more suitable for racing than touring. Conversely some riders might like the upright position of the flat bar bike with the short stem extension, but probably more from bad riding habits than from careful consideration of what feels best. The right back angle is critical for comfort. When you find it, choose a stem that lets you ride at that angle without strain.

# Wearing Glasses While Cycling

## David L. Smith, M.D.

Imagine for a moment that you are zinging down a curvy mountain road this summer, braking carefully into each turn, enjoying yourself immensely. Suddenly—SPLAT! There's a gnat in your eye. The next sounds that break the silence are those of your bike and your head making contact with the tree at the beginning of the next curve. It's a gruesome thought, isn't it?

Glasses have basically three functions, in order of decreasing importance:

To correct refractive disorders: including nearsightedness or myopia, farsightedness or hyperopia, astigmatism, and presbyopia (loss of near vision due to old age); to protect the eyes from flying objects and excessive sunlight; and decoration and camouflage, such as Elton John's latest frames or the window glass lenses worn by Clark (Superman) Kent.

When the eyes are exposed for several hours to bright light such as summer sunlight, the visual pigments in the retina are washed out, and the eyes function poorly when darkness falls. For this reason, wearing sunglasses is a good idea for any long rides during the day, even if the sun is not uncomfortably bright. Under extreme conditions, such as skiing on a sunny day, the eyeballs can even be sunburned.

There are two basic types of frames: plastic and metal. When the cyclist is bent over the bars, he or she tends to look through the very top part of the lens. For this reason, the frame should allow a large portion of the lens to sit above normal eye level, and the frame itself should be thin or nonexistent at the top, so that the frame will not interfere with vision.

Plastic frames can be very light, but metal frames are generally thinner and have nosepieces that are adjustable to allow the lenses to sit high on the nose. The best type of frame for the cyclist is the rimless metal type consisting of earpieces and a center bridge, with no actual frame around the lenses at all. The lenses can be any shape and size desired.

The following additional points are important in selecting frames: earpieces that wrap around the ear (cable type) do a better job of holding the glasses on the face, but are more likely to cause irritation behind the ears, especially with a heavy lens; other types of earpieces are usually satisfactory if used with a band around the back of the head to hold the glasses on. The nosepieces of metal glasses tend to dig into the nose. I recommend soft plastic cushions on the nosepiece, generally available in opticians' shops. The frame should cover a wide field of view and hold the lenses as close to the eye as possisble without discomfort. This will provide maximum protection and visual clarity.

There are two types of lenses: plastic and glass. Plastic lenses are much lighter and are the only way to go, except for contacts, for a person like myself who needs very thick lenses. Their disadvantage is that they are easily scratched. Fancy sunglass lenses such as Polaroid are, as of this writing, only made of glass. Glass lenses can shatter in an accident, but government standards for lenses make this possibility less likely than it used to be. For a person who does not need a thick prescription lens, the Polaroid or Photosun lenses are probably best. Polaroid lenses eliminate glare from road and water surfaces, while the Photosun-type lenses have a limited capacity to adjust to ambient light levels. However, I do not recommend that these or any sunglasses be used outdoors after sundown.

Sunglass lenses should be a smoke-colored, neutral gray. Green lenses are probably second best. Other colors, such as blue, yellow, or red, are not very good. Contact lenses are sexy, but make things worse if a foreign body (sand or bug) gets into the eye. In case of an accident, contact lens wearers should wear a Medic-Alert bracelet or medallion when out bicycling, since most contact lenses will injure the eye if left in for a long period of time.

The oculist has another trick up his sleeve that is of use to the cyclist: prism lenses. A prism lens of 15–20 diopters, mounted "base up," allows the cyclist to see ahead while looking down. Lenses for nearsighted people like me tend to have some of this effect built-in, while lenses for farsighted people have the opposite effect. A prism lens can be ground as part of the prescription, but a much lighter and more efficient solution is to use a paste-on Fresnel lens on top of the glasses you may already have. These paste-on Fresnel lenses can be specially ordered by the oculist.

# The Effects of Narrow Saddles on Male Cyclists

## Eugene A. Gaston, M.D.

The May 6, 1978, issue of *Lancet*, a top-quality British medical journal, contained a short article entitled "Bicycle Saddles and Torsion of the Testis" written by two English surgeons, R. H. Jackson and A. W. Craft. The article reported the cases of five boys, 13 to 15 years of age, each of whom required an emergency operation because the spermatic cord to one testicle (the terms testis and testicle are synonymous) had become twisted as the testicle rotated in the scrotal sac. Each of the boys was reported to have a "racing bicycle" with dropped handlebars and a "long narrow saddle which comes forward under the perineum and scrotum. It would appear that the testis becomes twisted between the thigh and the saddle as the legs go up and down. Presumably the dropped handlebars tend to bring the legs closer up to the abdomen and increase the compression of the scrotum and its contents against the saddle." The surgeons concluded that: "If such cases are common, these saddles ought to be redesigned."

No doubt Messrs. Jackson and Craft are excellent surgeons (English surgeons do not use the prefix Dr.), but they are almost certainly not experienced bicyclists. The purpose of this article is to bring the condition to the attention of our readers and to examine the evidence against narrow saddles and dropped handlebars.

Jackson and Craft made no estimate of the frequency with which rotation of the testicle is associated with bicycling, stating only that in the "past few years" they have seen five cases. During the same years, many other cases not related to bicycling probably had been seen at their hospital. Their collection of five cases is almost certainly a coincidence; if the patients had been distributed among five hospitals no one would have given the matter a second thought. Furthermore, in four of their five patients the association between torsion and bicycling was very tenuous. In only one patient did the testicular rotation occur when the boy was actually riding. In two others, the pain started at some unspecified time after rides, and the last two boys had simply obtained new bicycles a few days earlier.

The authors' theory that the "testis becomes twisted between the thigh and saddle as the legs go up and down" is unrealistic. Pain would soon put a stop to such activity, with or without rotation. Moreover, during exercise the dartos muscle, which lines the scrotum, contracts, pulling the testis up against the body out of harm's way. Introspection, plus conversations with other riders, confirms the importance of the dartos muscle and clothing, the latter often supplemented with an athletic supporter, in stabilizing the position of the scrotum. Even if this were not true, there is obviously insufficient room for the scrotum between the thigh and saddle regardless of whether the latter is long and narrow or short and wide. The position of the upper part of the body necessary to reach the drops on handlebars is obtained, not so much by forward rotation of the pelvis as by flexion of the lumbar spine. The position of the scrotum, in relation to the saddle and thighs, therefore remains relatively constant regardless of the riding position.

Is bicycle riding an unacceptable risk to those who have the developmental defect which allows rotation of the testicle to take place? The answer is no, even if such individuals could be identified before the event (which is impossible). If the testicle is not attached to the scrotum, it will probably eventually rotate regardless of activity. In a review of 101 cases seen at another English hospital* only six patients gave histories of "injuries or strains" of any kind preceding the onset of symptoms. The condition often comes on during sleep, when the patient rolls over but the testicle does not.

The chance of any one male having the congenital defect which allows the testicle to rotate is very small indeed. If you do have the defect, you will probably experience torsion regardless of your activity. Do not change your handlebars, saddle or riding style; just see a doctor at once should you suddenly get unexplained pain in a testicle, even if it is only transient. There are plenty of things to worry about when riding a bicycle such as traffic, dogs and broken glass. Torsion of the testicle should not be one of them.

# Interval Training

## John Schubert

You enjoy cycling, but you find that it doesn't give you a good workout like you get from running or racquetball. Or you get the

---

*R. H. Chapman and A. J. Walton, "Torsion of the Testis and Its Appendages," *British Medical Journal*, no. 1 (1972), pp. 164–66.

workout you want when you have enough time for a long ride, but you seldom have enough time. Or you want to get in shape for a long tour, a century ride, a quicker commuting time to work, your first race or your one-hundredth race.

Maybe you ought to try interval training.

Interval training offers benefits you'll never get from your ordinary rides, no matter how long or how hard they are. An interval workout can be over in less than an hour, giving you time for life's other demands. It will give you more leg speed, smoothness and hill-eating stamina. Your sense of pace will improve greatly.

Like the interval training a swimmer or runner does, a cyclist's interval workouts are serious business. To begin with, they're certainly less idyllic (and, to some people, less enjoyable) than a leisurely ride through the country. Like the runner who gets a pulled muscle or a swimmer who gets bursitis, a cyclist who undertakes intervals without getting in reasonably good shape first is likely to sustain an injury—typically, an inflammation of the knee or Achilles tendon. A cyclist is much more likely to benefit from interval workouts when coordinating them with an overall training plan. (Your overall plan may be as simple as alternating hard and easy workout days or a complicated schedule designed to make you peak for an event many months hence.)

Before you think about starting interval training, get in enough miles to acclimate your body (especially your joints and tendons) to the stresses of cycling. A month of steady riding, with a month's total of 300 miles, should be a strict minimum. (That may sound like a lot, but it's not; you can total 300 miles by taking 25 rides of 12 miles each.) During your month of steady riding, concentrate on becoming loose. Don't ever let yourself coast. Spin your feet smoothly and quickly in low gears. You should use gears low enough that you're barely conscious of exerting any force on the pedals. Anytime you find yourself slowing down, shift to a lower gear to keep your cadence (pedaling speed) high. And during this month, do some static stretching exercises every day.

The principle of interval workouts is simple: you ride hard for short work intervals and have a rest interval between your work intervals. During the work intervals, you maintain a level of effort that would tire you out if you didn't have a chance to recover in the rest interval. The high level of effort taxes your leg muscles and your cardiovascular system so they get stronger. Interval training is the fastest way to build up your aerobic fitness. (Track racers use exceptionally short intervals to build up their sprint speed, too.)

Your first workouts should be on a fairly flat road. (Later, you may want to ride intervals over varied terrain, but by restricting yourself to flat terrain at first, you'll develop a better sense of pace.)

Before you start any interval workout, ride steadily for 20 to 30 minutes to warm up. Then get off the bike and do your routine of static stretching exercises—but don't attempt stretching exercises now if you aren't used to them. Now is a very bad time to introduce yourself to stretching.

The work period in an interval workout can be as short as 30 seconds or as long as 15 minutes. Your first interval workouts should have three or four work periods about 5 minutes long, separated by a 3- or 4-minute rest period, and followed by 10 or 20 minutes of steady cycling to cool down.

The oft-quoted rule of thumb is that your pulse should climb to 180 beats per minute during the work interval and drop down to 120 during your rest period. If your pulse stays above 120, you should lengthen your rest periods. There's no virtue in attempting a workout you can't complete, or a workout that leaves you breathless and too tired to spin when you're halfway through. So don't feel shy about resting until you feel comfortable enough to ride another repetition of the work interval.

During the work interval, cycle at a higher cadence than you're used to. If you customarily ride with a cadence of 70 to 85 rpm (and you should be used to a cadence at least that fast if you've done your homework with that month of steady mileage), ride with a cadence of 100 to 110. This will probably be the fastest rate at which you can spin comfortably. If you're not blessed with superb coordination, you'll find your form deteriorating at cadences faster than this— which means it's too early to attempt them. (If you stay with interval training for a long time, however, you'll find yourself reaching for cadences of 150 or more.)

For your intervals to be successful, it's important that you use a low-enough gear to get through them. If you start out with a too-high gear, you won't be able to maintain the cadence you started with throughout all the workout's repetitions, and maintaining a high cadence is the most important part of the workout. So don't fall prey to the temptation to whiz by in high gears. A gear of 70 inches (52-tooth chainwheel × 20-tooth cog) is the highest you should consider using. A gear in the low 60s may well be a better choice. A gear that low may seem too easy when you start your workout, but bear with it; you'll soon find yourself breathing hard. When you're doing your last repetition, the lower gear will seem very appropriate. It will enable you to maintain the same speed and help you develop your sense of pace. In any interval workout, the first repetition seems easy. Subsequent repetitions, however, should make you feel like you're working hard.

During your rest intervals, don't get off the bike and lounge on the grass. Keep pedaling, smoothly and evenly, and, of course, in a very low gear. Otherwise, your legs will tighten up. Go slowly so you recover from the work interval.

Now that you've finished one workout, more will follow. Make yourself a schedule of workouts and adhere to it. Keep a training diary and record how the workouts make you feel.

Don't do more than three interval workouts in a week, and don't do two in a row. Separate them with days of long, easy rides. As you get used to intervals, you can use them to push yourself harder. Spin until it hurts and scoot up the hills during your workouts. But don't ride the same workout repeatedly, or you'll grow to dread it. Variety in your workouts will help you attack each one with new vigor.

For example: Mondays, do a greater number of repetitions, but don't work quite as hard during each repetition, and keep your rest period short. Wednesdays, work on a really fast cadence; keep the work intervals short and the rest intervals a bit longer so you can keep the cadence quick and spirited. Saturdays, do long, hard intervals with long rest periods.

Experiment to see what you like doing and alternate workouts you like with workouts that develop your weaker capabilities. Find a friend to do intervals with; you'll find them much easier that way. But don't draft each other. If traffic permits, ride your intervals side-by-side. Find a highway with mileposts, get a stopwatch, and ride interval two-mile and three-mile repetitions for time. Or, when riding with your friend, pass each other several times during the work interval. You'll build up your speed that way. There are countless ways to spice up an interval workout; invent some of your own. They'll help you become a better cyclist.

# The Art of Roller Riding

## Alice Nass

I had never seriously considered roller riding for winter training. My impression of the contraption was that it was meant only for bike racers and acrobats who were able to defy certain laws of nature. However, I found the wind, freezing rain, and snow to be three good reasons to reconsider.

Not knowing how to begin I asked Len Vreeland for some advice. Vreeland is an accomplished roller rider, having set a world's record for riding—717 miles in 24 hours.

Mitch Mandel and T. L. Gettings

**Roller riding can help you improve your pedal cadence and your condition—in the comfort of your home.**

I brought my bike into Len's shop where he keeps his rollers. The familiarity of using my own bike was comforting. Len steadied the bike for me as I got on and began to pedal. I held on desperately; so tight, in fact, that my knuckles were white. My death grip was causing the front wheel to shake. At that point I was sure I would have lost my balance if Len hadn't been holding the bike. He explained that it's much better not to resist the natural cadence or rhythm of the bike.

After a few minutes I became more relaxed, and Len let go of the handlebars, assuring me that he still had hold of the seat. I felt like a child learning to ride a bike for the first time. I was instructed to keep the handlebars straight ahead. For balancing it is easiest to try to maintain a smooth pedal stroke. Len kept reminding me that the real key to staying on was confidence.

Like any other sport, setting up a program varies from person to person. You don't need to start out in a high gear. Begin with a gear you are comfortable with and then gradually shift into the higher gears. Pedal at your own pace until you've warmed up to 90 rpm. With practice this shouldn't take more than five minutes or so to do. The rpm doesn't have to be precise. Len dangles a watch from his handlebars and counts his revolutions for 15 seconds. He then multiplies this by four to determine the approximate pedal rate. "I'll do 90 rpm after the five minute warm-up period. Then I'll do 100 rpm and just keep building on that. The more conditioned I am, the higher the rate I pedal. When I get to 120 rpm I try some wind sprints."

Your own program should fit your abilities starting with day one. If you are accustomed to coasting on your bike as much as pedaling, then you may want to begin in a low gear, doing fewer rpm for a shorter amount of time. Gradually you will find you can stay on longer and pedal faster.

Keeping a written record of your progress will be a good guide so you know how you are doing. As you improve you will be encouraged to keep it up. Some suggestions are to note the gear you are in, the time it takes to reach 90 rpm, and how long you can sustain increased revolutions. You can check your pulse rate. If your rollers have a speedometer/odometer attachment, record the miles ridden per day. Try sprinting. Working out on the rollers doesn't have to be boring. Make a game of it. Vary your program. Listen to the radio, watch television or contemplate the bleak outdoors. Just so you don't daydream and steer off the rollers. It does require a certain amount of concentration to keep pedaling.

Count rpm, time yourself, and keep a pedal cadence. This is better than setting a mileage goal. You will then derive the physical benefits you were after from the start. Those interested in track or roller racing can work on full sprints after the workout. Then see how long you can maintain a really high rpm.

Is roller riding of any real value? The benefits to the cardiovascular and respiratory systems are obvious. But you also learn how to better handle a bike for touring. You become a much smoother rider on the road after learning to ride high rpm on rollers. Len comments, "I've had people tell me over the years that they are amazed at how straight and fast I ride the bike on the road. The only way that you can ride high rpm on rollers is to ride perfectly straight or else you'll go off. So you just naturally develop this real smooth, circular-type pedaling. Rather than lunging down on each pedal you get a much more even power drive using a full pedal stroke."

After a few tries I managed to spin the wheels for about 20 minutes. In that short time I had worked up some steam. In fact, I was really sweating and ready to take a breather. But how do you get off rollers? As I slowed down, my balance was wavering. Len advised me to keep my front wheel pointed forward. If the bike is turned at an angle it will slip off. You can get a feel for the precise moment to step down. Or, as in my case, have someone there to hold onto the bike.

If you are alone and don't have anyone to coach you, set the rollers in a doorway so that your body is in the frame of the door. "Have a solid stool or chair on the side," Len suggests, "if you don't have mounting steps on your rollers. With shoulders faced to the doorway use the walls to keep your balance. Put one hand on the doorway and one on the handlebars as a crutch to gain confidence."

You'll learn quite a lot about yourself riding rollers. You'll remain in peak cycling condition, and come Spring, you just might be a better bike handler.

# Medical Q and A

When cycling distances in excess of 50 miles, I experience sharp pain at the bottom of the back of my neck on down through my shoulders. It is most certainly connected with fatigue in my arms and shoulders from supporting my weight on the dropped handlebars. I have talked with other riders who have experienced similar discomfort. They have stated that it is a matter of conditioning. However, I commute approximately 50 miles each week and may ride up to 70 miles on the weekends.

What is this pain I am experiencing, and how can I best condition myself to at least alleviate some of the irritation?

P. B. E., Dover, MA

I cannot be sure of the cause of your problem without having examined you, your cycling technique and position. Before you read any further, I would advise you to visit an orthopedic surgeon who can determine whether there is anything wrong with your neck or shoulders that could cause pain by pinching a nerve. Such problems could include a herniated cervical disk or a cervical rib (an extra, thirteenth rib above the position of the normal ribs, that can compress a nerve going under it). Sometimes old injuries such as pulled muscles can be aggravated by weight-bearing at the shoulders.

I suspect, however, that your problem is simply a result of the kind of load your arms and shoulder muscles are called upon to bear. A constant weight will fatigue a muscle much more quickly than a heavier load applied intermittently. At the same time, a constant weight-bearing situation without motion does less to condition the muscles than a situation in which intermittent heavy work is performed. To give an example, it is much more tiring to stand motionless for an hour than it is to walk or cycle briskly for that same hour, and of course at the end of the hour of standing motionless, no useful exercise has been performed.

To alleviate your condition, assuming there is nothing wrong with your bones, joints or nerves, I would suggest a twofold program:

Weight lift to strengthen the upper extremities. I would suggest lifting a moderate weight many times rather than struggling to lift a large weight once or a few times.

Change your cycling position to put more weight on your rear end and less on your front end. This can be accomplished by moving the seat forward, using a shorter extension, using randonneur bars, or raising the height of the stem.

David L. Smith, M.D.

I am 6 feet, 2 inches tall and am riding a 25½-inch bicycle. The saddle height of 109 percent of leg length seems to be fine, but when I ride long distances I get pain between the shoulder blades. The solution seems to be to raise the handlebars. To do this I need a longer stem, but so far have been unable to find one. Extensions vary in size, but stems all have the same length—too short.

M. M., College Park, MD

*The 25½-inch frame should be about right for you. The pain is probably due to maladjustment of saddle and bars relative to your build. You may be straining to reach the handlebars; try shortening the distance between saddle and bars by moving the saddle forward* or using a stem with a shorter extension. The saddle may be too high; the 109 percent rule is only a starting point for adjustment. Changing the angle of saddle, handlebar or both may solve the problem.

Eugene A. Gaston, M.D.

Last winter I had an inflammation of my right leg-to-hip ball joint. It might have been a touch of bursitis. My doctor gave me a shot there that calmed it down. Shortly after that I felt a mid-back, right-side muscle freeze up. It felt as if it were tied in a knot. Both problems lingered on with mild to not so mild discomfort for months.

I am 39 years old and regularly ride 50 miles a week, sometimes all out. I recently adjusted my saddle to 109 percent of my leg length. I'm not going to ride much for a while, although I do notice that the new position of the seat lets me use my bigger leg muscles more, with a possible lessening of back and pelvic twisting.

R. C., Worcester, MA

Placing the saddle at 109 percent of the inseam length above the pedal is not a hard and fast rule. It does not take into account the length of the feet or the tilt and flexibility of the saddle. Your back pain may be related to your posture while riding, and the height and the tilt of the saddle are important in determining posture. Other factors which may affect your back are the height of the handlebars and their distance from the saddle. Try adjusting all three until you find a comfortable combination. If your symptoms persist, daily calisthenics to stretch and limber up the ligaments and muscles of the back are worth trying.

Eugene A. Gaston, M.D.

I am 27 years old and like to ride long distances but am limited by lower back pain, which begins after I have ridden about 35 miles. I have never had back trouble before. I believe that part of the answer is to replace the stem that came with my 23-inch bicycle (it has a 95-mm extension) with one of shorter extension but greater length. My reasons are: after numerous adjustments over several months, I believe my saddle is now at optimal position; the distance from my elbow to my outstretched fingertips is 1½ inches shorter than the distance between the nose of the saddle and the handlebars; the handlebar is about 2 inches lower than the saddle when the stem is raised to the limit that still leaves enough in the fork tube to be safe; when I stand with my legs straddling the bicycle, there is barely an inch between the top tube and my crotch, so it is not a matter of getting a larger frame.

H. I., Queens Village, NY

*Your symptoms suggest postural backache due to the long reach of the handlebar. A new stem may be the answer, but with a normal size frame you probably have the saddle unnecessarily high. Try lowering it and pushing it forward. If your backache disappears, you will have avoided the nuisance and expense of installing a new system. Daily exercises to stretch the back muscles and ligaments may also help.*

Eugene A. Gaston, M.D.

I am 53 years old, 5 feet, 11 inches tall and weigh 165 pounds. I consider myself in excellent shape. I ride on a 50-mile round trip once or twice a week.

After 10 or 12 miles I develop a very sensitive and painful area at the upper interior end of the trapezius muscle on the left side only. The area, about the size of a quarter, is very painful to the touch and also if I bend my head forward.

As soon as I am off the bike and moving about the pain disappears and will only return after about ten miles on the bicycle.

What is the cause? Remember, it only affects the left side. Can I do anything to prevent this from recurring? Incidentally, I ride a 10-speed with down-turned handlebars.

S. S., Solana Beach, CA

*With down-turned handlebars, the weight of the head and upper chest is suspended from the arms via the shoulder muscles, especially the trapezius. This kind of constant load is very fatiguing. Pain and stiffness can be generalized or localized in an area of an old unremembered injury. I would suggest a weight-lifting program to strengthen the arms and shoulders. Changing the position of seat and handlebars to take weight off the arms may be helpful. (Of course, this can lead to pain lower down in the anatomy.) You should shift your hand and arm position frequently while riding. Use plenty of padding on the bars and wear gloves to absorb road shock. I would consider the use of upright bars only as a last resort.*

*Sometimes localized pain in the shoulders can be due to a pinched nerve, calcium deposits or almost anything under the sun including heart disease or gallstones. For localized pain, see your doctor first.*

David L. Smith, M.D.

I am a 23-year-old woman and find my efforts to become an avid bicyclist hindered by recurring pains. I have a 10-speed bike with drop handlebars and usually ride with my hands on the top of the bars and brake with the safety levers. After a half hour in this position I get pain between my shoulder blades and a dull ache in the lower back. When I ride with my hands on the drops I get pain in the back of the neck, and my vision is limited. My husband suggested that my muscles would eventually get stronger and the pain would disappear, but this has not happened even though I bike three times a week in the summer and use rollers more frequently in the winter. Raising and lowering the seat and adjusting the angle of the handlebars have not helped. Can you offer any suggestions before I give up?

M. M. M., River Forest, IL

*All athletic endeavors are associated with aches and pains which usually disappear when the body becomes acclimated to the new activity. Even professional athletes suffer at the beginning of each new season as they struggle to get in shape. Don't give up, you'll make it. Try shortening the distance between the saddle and the handlebars; the pains between the shoulder blades and in the lower back suggest that you are straining to reach the bars. Pain in the back of the neck when using the drops can be temporarily relieved by keeping the head down and raising the eyes, as when looking over the tops of glasses. Raising the handlebars in relation to the saddle helps, as does changing to randonneur bars which have less drop. Some excellent bicyclists have stopped using drop bars because of continued neck pain and get along well with upright bars, of which several styles are available.*

Eugene A. Gaston, M.D.

Two years ago, while wearing a hard-shell helmet, I fell striking my head. The inside liner of the helmet crushed and absorbed enough shock so that I had no concussion nor headache, but I did chip teeth and break my glasses. I recovered completely except for an injury to my neck, similar to whiplash, which prevents me from riding more than a few miles with the weight of the hard-shell helmet on my head. I still wear it around town but use a leather helmet on longer rides. On long tours I ride much of the way with my hands off the handlebars to keep my neck from hurting. I would like to ride long distances comfortably again. What do you suggest?

W. L., Columbia, SC

*I assume that X rays of the neck have ruled out fractures. The necessity for keeping the neck hyperextended to see the road ahead* while riding on the drops causes many riders to have neck pain. The accident added avulsion (tearing) injuries to your neck muscles. They have not healed because of the continuing trauma of your riding position. Rearrange your bike so you are in a more upright, comfortable position. Shorten the distance between bars and saddle and eliminate or lessen the degree of drop by changing bars. Gentle stretching exercises to the neck—forward, backward, to each side and twisting in both directions—done twice daily will help. You will eventually recover. In the meantine, continue to wear your helmet. It weighs less than 1½ pounds and probably prevented a much more serious injury.

Eugene A. Gaston, M.D.

I read about hand and seat difficulties in cycling, but I haven't read about foot problems as I have encountered using toe clips, straps and rattrap pedals. These items are most helpful in riding, but I have been forced to use rubber pedals due to pinching of toes and very substantial pain after prolonged use (ten miles) of toe clips and straps. I use regular street shoes. Do you have any remedy?

E. G. M., Arlington, VA

The clips are probably causing pressure in a top-to-bottom direction, and this is being transmitted to your toes through your normally comfortable street shoes. Try altering the shape of the clips so this does not happen, and keep the toe strap fairly loose.

Eugene A. Gaston, M.D.

After a recent bike ride I suffered severe pains in my right foot. The pain only occurred when I had ridden up steep inclines. It never hurts while riding, only after I have stopped. The pain is on the outside edge of my right foot, and there seems to be an enlarged bone where the pain originates. The pain is normally a throbbing sensation and only lasts for a few minutes, then disappears.

A. B., Melbourne, Australia

If the pain and apparent bone were present on the inside of the foot, near the big toe, I would say that you had a bunion, which is a disease of the first joint of the big toe. I think your case must be similar, but with the problem in or near the first joint of the little toe. This sort of thing can be caused by too tight shoes or toe straps, together with jamming the toes down into the end of the shoe during hard pedaling. I would try the following measures to take all pressure off the affected area while riding:

Make sure that your riding shoes are wide enough. The Italian shoes are often too narrow. You might want to cut a two-centimeter hole in the side of the shoe over the area.

Do not tighten the toe straps so much that the toes are squeezed together.

Try a narrow platform pedal which allows the outside of the foot to ride completely free.

Any overlying callouses should be shaved down by a podiatrist.

Alter your pedaling style. Use lower gears and go up the hills without having to bear down so heavily. Make sure that your saddle is high enough so that your legs have run out of travel by the bottom of the stroke.

David L. Smith, M.D.

I have cycled moderately for the past nine years with no problems. This Christmas I received a set of rollers and have had sore knees since. Why should rollers cause sore knees and not regular cycling, and how do I correct it?

C. W. C., Springfield, PA

It would help to know your age; the location of the pain; the type and pressure of your tires; the gear you are using; and the duration, speed and frequency of your roller sessions. Roller riding is bereft of downhill rests and requires harder pushing with higher gears and softer tires. Your problem may be the result of pushing harder for longer periods of time, and doing it more frequently than with regular cycling. It may also be related to a different stance on the bicycle. Check the positions of your feet on the pedals, the height of the saddle and handlebars and their positions in relation to each other. With a little experimenting you can probably find the answer.

Eugene A Gaston, M.D.

I am 15 years old, weigh 150 pounds and am 5 feet, 8 inches tall. I would like to race and have a set of rollers. Over the winter I would like to perfect my cadence. Could you please explain how and also what is the correct rpm for racing?

F. M., Highland Park, IL

When we're talking of rpm, the term refers to revolutions per minute. For the competitive rider, rpm between 90 to 115 are commonly used, although these values will be exceeded during sprints and reduced somewhat in hill climbing. A satisfactory roller workout would maintain a cadence of 100 to 110 rpm with periodic increases, 30 to 60 seconds at higher rpm.

David L. Smith, M.D.